BLS WORKING PAPERS

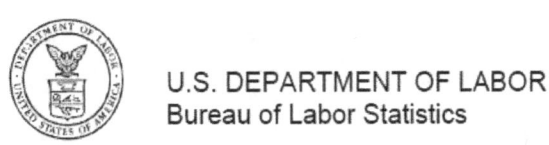

U.S. DEPARTMENT OF LABOR
Bureau of Labor Statistics

OFFICE OF PRICES AND LIVING
CONDITIONS

A Complete Characterization of the Implications of Slutzky Symmetry for the Linear, Log-Linear, and Semi-Log Incomplete Demand System Models

Roger H. von Haefen, U.S. Bureau of Labor Statistics

Working Paper 332
September 2000

A Complete Characterization of the Implications of Slutsky Symmetry for the Linear, Log-Linear, and Semi-Log Incomplete Demand System Models

Roger H. von Haefen[†]
Research Economist
Division of Price and Index Number Research
U.S. Bureau of Labor Statistics
Room 3105
2 Massachusetts Ave, NE
Washington, DC 20212
Phone – (202) 691-6593
Fax – (202) 691-6583
Von_Haefen_R@bls.gov

First Draft – March 17, 2000
Revised – July 20, 2000

[†] I would like to thank V. Kerry Smith and J. Scott Shonkwiler for helpful comments on earlier drafts of this paper. All remaining errors are my own responsibility.

Abstract

This paper extends previous research by LaFrance [1985, 1986, 1987] by deriving the necessary parameter restrictions for two additional classes of incomplete demand system models to have symmetric Slutsky substitution matrices in a local neighborhood of price and income values. In contrast to LaFrance's previous research, this paper considers models that treat expenditures and expenditure shares as the dependent variables in the specified incomplete demand systems. Along with the eight models considered by LaFrance, the sixteen alternative specifications considered here represent a complete characterization of the implications of Slutsky symmetry for the linear, log-linear, and semi-log incomplete demand system models.

I.   *Introduction*

In a series of papers, LaFrance [1985, 1986, 1990] derives the necessary restrictions for the linear, log-linear, and semi-log incomplete demand system specifications to have symmetric Slutsky matrices in an open neighborhood of relevant price and income levels. These models employ the quantities demanded by the individual as the dependent variables in the specified demand equations, share a common linear-in-parameters and additive structure, and have been extensively used in applied work (e.g., Englin, Boxall, and Watson [1998], Shonkwiler [1999]). This paper extends LaFrance's results by examining the implications of Slutsky symmetry for sixteen additional incomplete demand system models. In contrast to the specifications considered by LaFrance, these structures treat the individual's expenditures and expenditure shares on the goods of interest as the dependent variables. Although complete expenditure and expenditure share demand systems models are frequently employed in empirical work, incomplete expenditure and expenditure share systems have received far less use. This paper's objective is to introduce to applied researchers a menu of theoretically consistent incomplete demand system specifications that employ expenditures and expenditure shares as the dependent variables. The necessary parameter restrictions for the linear, log-linear, and six variations of the semi-log expenditure and expenditure share models are derived. When closed form solutions exist, the quasi-indirect utility functions for the restricted demand models are also derived. Along with LaFrance's earlier work, the new results presented in this paper give a complete characterization of the implications of Slutsky symmetry for the linear, log-linear, and semi-log incomplete demand system models.

The paper is organized as follows. The next section reviews the theory of incomplete demand systems. Section III presents the necessary parameter restrictions, the implied structure of the expenditure and expenditure share models, and the structures of the quasi-indirect utility functions when closed form solutions exist. For completeness, results for the eight models considered by LaFrance are also presented. Because the necessary restrictions for Slutsky symmetry to hold in an open neighborhood of price and income levels are generally found to be quite restrictive, the paper concludes with a discussion of the relative merits of imposing Slutsky symmetry in an open neighborhood versus at a single set of price and income values.

II.   *Incomplete Demand Systems*

Applied researchers are often interested in modeling the demand for a subset of goods entering an individual's preference ordering. To consistently model consumption for these goods within a demand systems framework, the analyst may employ one of three sets of assumptions. One approach assumes the goods of interest enter consumer preferences through a weakly separable subfunction. In this case, the analyst models consumption for the goods of interest conditional on total expenditures allocated to them. Alternatively, the analyst may assume that the other goods' prices vary proportionately across individuals and/or time. In this situation, the other goods can be aggregated into a single Hicksian composite good, and the analyst models the demand for the goods of interest as functions of their prices, total income, and the composite good's price index. A third approach involves the specification of a demand system for the goods of interest as functions of their own prices, total income, and the other goods' prices that are assumed quasi-fixed. This latter strategy falls under the rubric of incomplete demand system approaches and has been systematically investigated by Epstein [1982] and LaFrance and Hanemann [1989].

The incomplete demand system framework assumes that consumer demand for a set of n goods can be represented by the following system of Marshallian demand functions:

$$x_i = x_i(\boldsymbol{p}, \boldsymbol{q}, y, \beta), i = 1, \ldots, n \tag{1}$$

where x_i is the Marshallian consumer's demand for good i, $\boldsymbol{p}$ is a vector of prices for the n goods in (1), $\boldsymbol{q}$ is a vector of prices for m other goods whose demands are not explicitly specified, y is the consumer's income, and $\boldsymbol{\beta}$ is a vector of structural parameters. Following LaFrance [1985, 1986, 1990], $\boldsymbol{p}$, $\boldsymbol{q}$, and y are all normalized by $\pi(\boldsymbol{q})$, a homogenous of degree one price index for the m other goods, to insure the demand equations are homogeneous of degree zero in prices and income. It is because the analyst models the demand for the n goods in $\boldsymbol{x}$ as functions of all $n + m$ prices and income that the demand specification in (1) is incomplete.

In principle, the analyst can generate (1) by either: 1) specifying an indirect utility function and using Roy's Identity; or (2) specifying the system of incomplete demand equations directly. With either approach, a significant question for analysts attempting to use (1) to generate consistent Hicksian welfare measures for a set of price changes is whether the system is consistent with a rational individual maximizing her utility subject to a linear budget constraint. This is the classic integrability problem. As noted by LaFrance and Hanemann [1989], there are at least three distinct concepts of integrability in the incomplete demand systems framework. This paper employs LaFrance and Hanemann's concept of weak integrability. This concept implies that within a local neighborhood of price and income values, there exists a continuous and increasing preference ordering that both gives rise to and is quasiconcave in $\boldsymbol{x}$ and s, where s is defined as total expenditures on the m other goods, i.e., $s = y - \sum_{i=1}^{n} p_i x_i$. Compared to other concepts of integrability in an incomplete demand systems framework, weak integrability represents the minimal set of assumptions that allow the analyst to construct exact welfare measures for changes in $\boldsymbol{p}$ conditional on quasifixed values of $\boldsymbol{q}$.

Theorem 2 in LaFrance and Hanemann states that an incomplete demand system is weakly integrable if the following four conditions are satisfied: 1) $\boldsymbol{x}$ is homogenous of degree zero in prices and income; 2) $\boldsymbol{x}$ is nonnegative, i.e., $\boldsymbol{x} \geq 0$; 3) expenditures on the n goods included in the incomplete demand system are strictly less than income, i.e., $\sum_{i=1}^{n} p_i x_i < y$; and

4) the Slutsky substitution matrix, i.e., the $n \times n$ matrix whose elements consist of:

$$s_{ij} = \frac{\partial x_i}{\partial p_j} + \frac{\partial x_i}{\partial y} x_j, \, i, j \in 1,...,n \tag{2}$$

where $\partial x_i / \partial p_j$ and $\partial x_i / \partial y$ are partial derivatives of the Marshallian demand functions with respect to price and income, respectively, is symmetric and negative semidefinite. Symmetry is accomplished if for each good $i, j \in n$, $i \neq j$, $s_{ij} = s_{ji}$, whereas negative semidefiniteness requires that the Slutsky matrix's eigenvalues are nonpositive. The normalization of prices and income by the price index, $\pi(q)$, implies that the first condition is satisfied, and the second and third conditions are innocuous in many applied situations and assumed to hold in an open neighborhood of prices and income. Thus, the necessary conditions for weak integrability that imply added structure for (1) are the symmetry and negative semidefiniteness of the Slutsky matrix.

In a series of papers, LaFrance derives the necessary parameter restrictions for the Slutsky matrix to be symmetric for eight incomplete demand system specifications – the linear model [1985], the log-linear or constant elasticity model [1986], and six alternative semi-log models [1990]. These models or their logarithmic transformations share a common linear-in-parameters structure and are additive in their arguments. Table 1 lists the eight demand specifications LaFrance considers. This paper extends his results by deriving the implications of Slutsky symmetry for two additional classes of incomplete demand system models. Sixteen additional specifications are considered that treat either expenditures ($e_i = p_i x_i, e_i > 0$), expenditure shares ($s_i = p_i x_i / y, 0 < s_i < 1$), or their logarithmic transformations as the dependent variables. Tables 2 and 3 list the expenditure and expenditure share specifications considered in this paper.

In addition to expanding the menu of specifications from which analysts can choose, these models may be of interest to applied researchers for at least two additional reasons. Since Stone's [1954a, 1954b] pioneering work, it has been common in applied demand analysis for expenditures, expenditure shares, or transformations of them to be specified as the dependent variables in the estimated system of equations. Three of the most widely used empirical specifications, the linear expenditure system (Klein and Rubin [1947-1948]), the Indirect Translog (Christensen, Jorgenson, and Lau [1975]), and the Almost Ideal Demand System (Deaton and Muellbauer [1980]), treat expenditures or expenditure shares as the system's dependent variables. Furthermore, many of the expenditure and expenditure share structures explored here may be of interest to researchers estimating dual specifications of generalized corner solution models (Bockstael, Hanemann, and Strand [1986]), i.e., demand systems that consistently account for the presence of both interior and corner solutions. At present, empirical specification of these models proposed by Lee and Pitt [1986] and recently implemented by Phaneuf [1999] only consider *complete* or weakly separable demand systems, but these models can also be estimated within an incomplete demand system framework.[1] Moreover, the implementation of the dual models proposed by Lee and Pitt depend critically on the existence of closed form solutions for the implied virtual price functions, i.e., the prices that would drive the consumer's demand for the nonconsumed goods to zero (Neary and Roberts [1980]). Because LaFrance's (x1)-(x4) specifications and the proposed (e1)-(e4) and (s1)-(s4) structures allow for corner solutions and have p entering linearly or log-linearly, they can in principle be inverted to solve for the implied virtual price functions.

For any pair of goods $i, j \in i,...,n; i \neq j$, the Slutsky symmetry restrictions require that in an open neighborhood of prices and income, the following conditions must hold for the demand, expenditure, and expenditure share equations, respectively:

---

[1] See von Haefen [2000] for a discussion of some practical issues associated with estimating these models.

$$\frac{\partial x_j}{\partial p_i} + \frac{\partial x_j}{\partial y} x_i = \frac{\partial x_i}{\partial p_j} + \frac{\partial x_i}{\partial y} x_j \tag{3}$$

$$\frac{1}{p_i p_j}\left[\frac{\partial e_j}{\partial p_i} p_i + \frac{\partial e_j}{\partial y} e_i\right] = \frac{1}{p_i p_j}\left[\frac{\partial e_i}{\partial p_j} p_j + \frac{\partial e_i}{\partial y} e_j\right] \tag{4}$$

$$\frac{y}{p_i p_j}\left[\frac{\partial s_j}{\partial p_i} p_i + \left\{\frac{s_j}{y} + \frac{\partial s_j}{\partial y}\right\} y s_i\right] = \frac{y}{p_i p_j}\left[\frac{\partial s_i}{\partial p_j} p_j + \left\{\frac{s_i}{y} + \frac{\partial s_i}{\partial y}\right\} y s_j\right] \tag{5}$$

where all derivatives are with respect to the Marshallian demands, expenditures, and expenditure shares, respectively. Table 4 reports the structure of these restrictions for the eight demand specifications explored by LaFrance, and Tables 5 and 6 report the restrictions for the sixteen expenditure and share models from Tables 2 and 3, respectively.

In addition to ascertaining the necessary parameter restrictions implied by Slutsky symmetry, determining whether the restricted demand systems can be linked to closed form representations of preferences may be of interest to applied researchers. For example, virtually every recently proposed method for linking intensive and extensive margins of consumer choice in a behaviorally consistent framework (e.g., Cameron [1992], Eom and Smith [1994]) assumes that consumer preferences can be represented by a utility function with a closed form solution. Without the closed form, these strategies would not be econometrically viable.

As noted by LaFrance and Hanemann [1989], a difficulty with the incomplete demand system framework is that one cannot recover the complete structure of preferences with respect to all $n + m$ goods from an n-good demand system that satisfies the conditions for weak integrability. However, one can recover what Hausman [1981] has called the *quasi*-indirect utility function by solving a series of partial differential equations. For the demand, expenditure, and expenditure share models, this can be accomplished sequentially by first solving one of the following partial differential equations:

$$\frac{\partial E(\cdot)}{\partial p_1} = x_1(\boldsymbol{p}, \boldsymbol{q}, E(\cdot), \boldsymbol{\beta}) \tag{6}$$

$$\frac{\partial E(\cdot)}{\partial \ln p_1} = e_1(\boldsymbol{p}, \boldsymbol{q}, E(\cdot), \boldsymbol{\beta}) \tag{7}$$

$$\frac{\partial \ln E(\cdot)}{\partial \ln p_1} = s_1(\boldsymbol{p}, \boldsymbol{q}, E(\cdot), \boldsymbol{\beta}) \tag{8}$$

where $E(\cdot)$ is the expenditure function evaluated at the baseline utility, $\overline{U}$, and good 1 is chosen arbitrarily with no loss in generality. In some cases, the techniques of differential calculus can be used to derive closed form solutions for $E(\cdot)$ (or $\ln E(\cdot)$) up to a constant of integration, $K_1(\overline{U}, \overline{\boldsymbol{p}}^{-1}, \boldsymbol{q})$, where $\overline{\boldsymbol{p}}^{-1}$ is the price vector for the $n-1$ remaining goods in the specified incomplete demand system. Because the constant of integration depends on the $n-1$ other prices, one can recover additional information about the structure of the expenditure function by sequentially solving the following differential equations for $i = 2, \ldots, n$:

$$\frac{\partial \widetilde{E}(\cdot)}{\partial p_i} + \frac{\partial K_{i-1}(\cdot)}{\partial p_i} = x_i(\boldsymbol{p}, \boldsymbol{q}, E(\cdot), \boldsymbol{\beta}) \tag{9}$$

$$\frac{\partial \widetilde{E}(\cdot)}{\partial \ln p_i} + \frac{\partial K_{i-1}(\cdot)}{\partial \ln p_i} = e_i(\boldsymbol{p}, \boldsymbol{q}, E(\cdot), \boldsymbol{\beta}) \tag{10}$$

$$\frac{\partial \ln \widetilde{E}(\cdot)}{\partial \ln p_i} + \frac{\partial K_{i-1}(\cdot)}{\partial \ln p_i} = s_i(\boldsymbol{p}, \boldsymbol{q}, E(\cdot), \boldsymbol{\beta}) \tag{11}$$

where $K_{i-1}(\cdot)$ is the constant of integration arising from the evaluation of the first $i-1$ partial differential equations and $\widetilde{E}(\cdot)$ is the identified component of the individual's expenditure function (i.e., that portion of the expenditure function excluding the constant of integration).

When the analyst has solved all n differential equations, the individual's expenditure function is identified up to the constant of integration, $K_n(\overline{U}, \boldsymbol{q})$, which is independent of $\boldsymbol{p}$. The fact that the constant of integration is a function of the baseline utility as well as the other m

goods' prices suggests that the analyst cannot identify the full structure of the expenditure function with respect to all $n + m$ goods from an incomplete demand system. However, one can obtain the quasi-indirect utility function by treating $K_n(\overline{U}, q)$ as the quasi-baseline utility and inverting, i.e.:

$$\tilde{U} = K_n(\overline{U}, q) = \phi(p, q, y, \beta) \tag{12}$$

LaFrance and Hanemann formally demonstrate that $\phi(p, q, y, \beta)$ can be used to consistently evaluate the welfare implications of one or several price changes for the n goods.

II.   Necessary Parameter Restrictions, the Structure of the Restricted Demand Systems, and the Quasi-Indirect Utility Functions

Tables 7, 8, and 9 reports all possible combinations of parameter restrictions that satisfy Slutsky symmetry for the demand, expenditure, and share specifications reported in Tables 1, 2, and 3, respectively.[2] The results in Table 7 were reported originally in LaFrance [1985, 1986, 1990] and are presented here mainly for completeness.[3] For expositional purposes, these tables employ some simplifying notation used by LaFrance. Let J, K, and N denote index sets satisfying $\emptyset \subset J \subset K \subset N \equiv \{1, 2, ..., n\}$, and let $\sim$ denote set differences, e.g., $N \sim J \equiv \{i \in N; i \notin J\}$. Further assume that if $J \neq \emptyset$, $1 \in J$, or if $K \neq \emptyset$, $1 \in K$.

The derivation of these results follows the logic laid out in LaFrance [1985, 1986]. For each specification, three mutually exclusive and exhaustive types of income effects for goods i and j are considered: 1) no income effects, i.e., $\gamma_i = \gamma_j = 0$; 2) both goods having income

---

[2] A technical appendix with the derivations for the expenditure and expenditure share parameter restrictions can be obtained from the author upon request. The appendix also contains derivations for LaFrance's (x2)-(x7) models, and the interested reader can consult LaFrance [1985, 1986] for the derivations of the (x1) and (x8) specifications.

effects, i.e., $\gamma_i \neq 0; \gamma_j \neq 0$; 2) only one good having income effects, ($\gamma_i \neq 0; \gamma_j = 0$). For each

of these possibilities, the necessary parameter restrictions for Slutsky symmetry to hold in an

open neighborhood of relevant prices and income were derived. The derivative properties of the

Slutsky symmetry conditions were used extensively to identify these parameter restrictions.

Because equations (4), (5), and (6) are assumed to hold over a range of price and income values,

they are identities that can be differentiated to generate additional restrictions. Theorem 2 in

LaFrance and Hanemann [1989]) identifies the following two equalities:

$$\frac{\partial s_{ij}}{\partial p_k} = \frac{\partial s_{ji}}{\partial p_k}, \quad i, j, k \in 1, ..., n; i \neq j \tag{13}$$

$$\frac{\partial s_{ij}}{\partial y} = \frac{\partial s_{ji}}{\partial y}, \quad i, j \in 1, ..., n; i \neq j \tag{14}$$

One should note, however, that these equalities are only a subset of the restrictions that can be

generated by differentiating the Slutsky symmetry identities. In principle, one can multiply

and/or add the same functions of market prices and income to both sides of the Slutsky symmetry

conditions and still preserve the identity relationship. One can then differentiate these modified

Slutsky identities to generate additional equalities that may help to identify the necessary

parameter restrictions. Once the parameter restrictions were identified for the three distinct

income relationships, consistent combinations of the three sets of parameter restrictions were then

determined, and the results are reported in Tables 7, 8, and 9.

    To help clarify the implications of the parameter restrictions reported in Tables 7, 8, and

9, Tables 10, 11, and 12 present the structure of the restricted incomplete demand systems. Not

all cross equation restrictions within sets of good can be represented in the restricted demand

specifications, so these tables should only be interpreted as suggestive of the general structure.

Tables 13, 14, and 15 also present the structure of the quasi-indirect utility functions for all

---

[3] A review of the results reported in LaFrance [1990] uncovered minor extensions for the (x5) and (x6)
specifications as well as a few typographical errors for the remaining specifications. The results reported in

restricted models with closed form solutions. These tables suggest that roughly one-half of the restricted models can be linked to closed form representation of consumer preferences.

Collectively, the results reported in Tables 7 through 15 imply that none of the twenty-four structures considered in this paper allow for both flexible income and Marshallian cross-price effects, and some do not allow for either. Perhaps the most general specifications are the (s3-1) and (s4-1) models that allow for general cross price effects but restrictively assume that all consumer demand equations are homothetic in income. Collectively, these findings suggest that strong and in many cases implausible assumptions about the structure of consumer preferences are required for analysts employing linear, semi-log, and log-linear incomplete demand system models.

III.   Discussion

This paper has extended LaFrance's earlier research by identifying the necessary parameter restrictions for systems of linear-in-parameters incomplete expenditure and expenditure share equations to satisfy the integrability condition of Slutsky symmetry. Although Slutsky symmetry is a necessary condition for the existence of a rational underlying preference ordering, it is not sufficient. As noted in Section II, integrability also requires that the Slutsky matrix must be negative semidefinite, i.e., the matrix's eigenvalues must be nonpositive. Imposing this later condition is confounded because the Slutsky matrix's elements are in general nonlinear functions of prices, income, and the demand system's structural parameters. As a result, the Slutsky matrix may not be negative semidefinite over the full range of relevant price and income values for the welfare scenarios under consideration.

Existing approaches to imposing curvature restrictions on systems of equations can be grouped into two broad categories: 1) those that impose negative semidefiniteness of the Slutsky

---

Tables 7, 10, and 13 incorporate these extensions and correct for the errors.

matrix at a single point (such as the each individual's observed prices and income or the sample average of these values); and 2) those that impose negative semidefiniteness globally over the full range of relevant price and income values through parameter restrictions (see Pitt and Millimet [2000] and Diewert and Wales [1987] for discussions of existing approaches). Although the latter approach is similar in spirit to the strategy for insuring Slutsky symmetry described in this paper, the former suggests a conceptually different strategy. In principle, the analyst could use the conditions in Tables 4, 5, and 6 as binding nonlinear constraints evaluated at the observed market price and income values when estimating the structural parameters of the demand equations. Although estimation of a system of equations subject to side constraints can be computationally burdensome, the approach has some precedence in the existing literature (LaFrance [1991]) and has both advantages and drawbacks. On the one hand, the results presented in the previous sections strongly suggest that imposing Slutsky symmetry on linear-in-parameters demand, expenditure, and expenditure share systems greatly limits the analyst's ability to allow for flexible income and Marshallian cross price effects. Imposing symmetry on the Slutsky matrix at a single point allows the analyst to incorporate these effects while preserving some degree of theoretical consistency. On the other hand, economists interested in using the estimated system of equations to evaluate the welfare implications of nonmarginal price changes may find it troubling that the model is capable of generating only approximate Hicsian values. Moreover, because symmetry of the Slutsky matrix is not preserved over the entire range of the relevant price changes, the approximate welfare measures are not independent of the ordering of the price changes.[4] Although these factors suggest that imposing Slutsky symmetry at a single point does not strictly dominate the approach pursued in this paper, it may be preferable with some applications.

---

[4] See LaFrance [1991] for a possible resolution to this problem.

References

Bockstael, Nancy, W. Michael Hanemann, and Ivar Strand [1986]: *Measuring the Benefits of Water Quality Improvements Using Recreation Demand Models*. Draft Report Presented to the US Environmental Protection Agency under Cooperative Agreement CR-811043-01-0, Washington, DC.

Cameron, Trudy Ann [1992]: "Combining Contingent Valuation and Travel Cost Data for the Valuation of Nonmarket Goods," *Land Economics*, 68(3): 302-317.

Christensen, Laurits, Dale Jorgenson, and Lawrence Lau [1975]: "Transcendental Logarithmic Utility Functions," *American Economic Review*, 65(3): 367-383.

Deaton, Angus, and John Muellbauer [1980]: "An Almost Ideal Demand System," *American Economic Review*, 70(3): 312-326.

Diewert, Erwin, and Terrance Wales [1987]: "Flexible Functional Forms and Global Curvature Conditions," *Econometrica*, 55(1): 43-68.

Englin, Jeffrey, Peter Boxall, and David Watson [1998]: "Modeling Recreation Demand in a Poisson System of Equations: An Analysis of the Impact of International Exchange Rates," *American Journal of Agricultural Economics*, 80(2): 255-263.

Eom, Young Sook, and V. Kerry Smith [1994]: "Calibrated Nonmarket Valuation," Working Paper, Department of Agricultural Economics, North Carolina State University.

Epstein, Larry [1982]: "Integrability of Incomplete Systems of Demand Functions," *Review of Economic Studies*, 49(3): 411-425.

Klein, Lawrence, and Herman Rubin [1947-1948]: "A Constant Utility Index of the Cost of Living," *Review of Economic Studies*, 15(2): 84-87.

Hausman, Jerry [1981]: "Éxact Consumer's Surplus and Deadweight Loss," *American Economic Review*, 71(4): 662-676.

LaFrance, Jeffrey [1985]: "Linear Demand Functions in Theory and Practice," *Journal of Economic Theory*, 37(1): 147-166.

LaFrance, Jeffrey [1986]: "The Structure of Constant Elasticity Demand Models," *American Journal of Agricultural Economics*, 68(3): 543-552.

LaFrance, Jeffrey [1990]: "Incomplete Demand Systems and Semilogarithmic Demand Models," *Australian Journal of Agricultural Economics*, 34(2): 118-131.

LaFrance, Jeffrey [1991]: "Consumer's Surplus versus Compensating Variation Revisited," *American Journal of Agricultural Economics*, 73(5): 1496-1507.

LaFrance, Jeffrey, and W. Michael Hanemann [1989]: "The Dual Structure of Incomplete Demand Systems," *American Journal of Agricultural Economics*, 71(2): 262-274.

Lee, Lung-Fei, and Mark Pitt [1986]: "Microeconomic Demand Systems with Binding Nonnegativity Constraints: The Dual Approach," *Econometrica*, 54(5): 1237-1242.

Neary, J.P., and K.W.S. Roberts [1980]: "The Theory of Household Behavior Under Rationing," *European Economic Review*, 13: 25-42.

Phaneuf, Daniel [1999]: "A Dual Approach to Modeling Corner Solutions in Recreation Demand," *Journal of Environmental Economics and Management*, 37(1): 85-105.

Pitt, Mark, and Daniel Millimet [2000]: "Estimation of Coherent Demand Systems with Many Binding Non-Negativity Constraints," Working Paper, Department of Economics, Brown University.

Shonkwiler, J. Scott [1999]: "Recreation Demand Systems for Multiple Site Count Data Travel Cost Models," in *Valuing Recreation and the Environment*, Catherine Kling and Joe Herriges, Editors, Northampton, MA: Edward Elgar.

Stone, Richard [1954a]: *The Measurement of Consumer's Expenditure and Behavior in the United Kingdom, 1920-1938, Vol. I*, Cambridge University Press.

Stone, Richard [1954b]: "Linear Expenditure Systems and Demand Analysis: An Application to the Pattern of British Demand," *Economic Journal*, 64(255): 511-527.

von Haefen, Roger [2000]: "Incomplete Demand Systems, Corner Solutions, and Welfare Measurement," Working Paper, Division of Price and Index Number Research, Bureau of Labor Statistics.

Table 1
Incomplete Demand System Models[1]

(x1) $\quad x_i = \alpha_i(\boldsymbol{q}) + \sum_{k=1}^{n} \beta_{ik} p_k + \gamma_i y$

(x2) $\quad x_i = \alpha_i(\boldsymbol{q}) + \sum_{k=1}^{n} \beta_{ik} p_k + \gamma_i \ln y$

(x3) $\quad x_i = \alpha_i(\boldsymbol{q}) + \sum_{k=1}^{n} \beta_{ik} \ln p_k + \gamma_i y$

(x4) $\quad x_i = \alpha_i(\boldsymbol{q}) + \sum_{k=1}^{n} \beta_{ik} \ln p_k + \gamma_i \ln y$

(x5) $\quad x_i = \alpha_i(\boldsymbol{q}) \exp\left\{ \sum_{k=1}^{n} \beta_{ik} p_k + \gamma_i y \right\}$

(x6) $\quad x_i = \alpha_i(\boldsymbol{q}) \exp\left\{ \sum_{k=1}^{n} \beta_{ik} p_k \right\} y^{\gamma_i}$

(x7) $\quad x_i = \alpha_i(\boldsymbol{q}) \prod_{k=1}^{n} p_k^{\beta_{ik}} \exp(\gamma_i y)$

(x8) $\quad x_i = \alpha_i(\boldsymbol{q}) \prod_{k=1}^{n} p_k^{\beta_{ik}} y^{\gamma_i}$

---

[1] The (x1) model is considered by LaFrance [1985], the (x2)-(x7) models are considered by LaFrance [1990] and coincide with models (m3), (m1), (m2), (m4), (m5), and (m6), respectively, and the (x8) model is studied in LaFrance [1985].

Table 2
Incomplete Expenditure System Models

(e1) $\quad e_i = \alpha_i(\boldsymbol{q}) + \sum_{k=1}^{n} \beta_{ik} p_k + \gamma_i y$

(e2) $\quad e_i = \alpha_i(\boldsymbol{q}) + \sum_{k=1}^{n} \beta_{ik} p_k + \gamma_i \ln y$

(e3) $\quad e_i = \alpha_i(\boldsymbol{q}) + \sum_{k=1}^{n} \beta_{ik} \ln p_k + \gamma_i y$

(e4) $\quad e_i = \alpha_i(\boldsymbol{q}) + \sum_{k=1}^{n} \beta_{ik} \ln p_k + \gamma_i \ln y$

(e5) $\quad e_i = \alpha_i(\boldsymbol{q}) \exp \left\{ \sum_{k=1}^{n} \beta_{ik} p_k + \gamma_i y \right\}$

(e6) $\quad e_i = \alpha_i(\boldsymbol{q}) \exp \left\{ \sum_{k=1}^{n} \beta_{ik} p_k \right\} y^{\gamma_i}$

(e7) $\quad e_i = \alpha_i(\boldsymbol{q}) \prod_{k=1}^{n} p_k^{\beta_{ik}} \exp(\gamma_i y)$

(e8) $\quad e_i = \alpha_i(\boldsymbol{q}) \prod_{k=1}^{n} p_k^{\beta_{ik}} y^{\gamma_i}$

Table 3
Incomplete Expenditure Share System Models

(s1) $\quad s_i = \alpha_i(\boldsymbol{q}) + \sum_{k=1}^{n} \beta_{ik} p_k + \gamma_i y$

(s2) $\quad s_i = \alpha_i(\boldsymbol{q}) + \sum_{k=1}^{n} \beta_{ik} p_k + \gamma_i \ln y$

(s3) $\quad s_i = \alpha_i(\boldsymbol{q}) + \sum_{k=1}^{n} \beta_{ik} \ln p_k + \gamma_i y$

(s4) $\quad s_i = \alpha_i(\boldsymbol{q}) + \sum_{k=1}^{n} \beta_{ik} \ln p_k + \gamma_i \ln y$

(s5) $\quad s_i = \alpha_i(\boldsymbol{q}) \exp\left\{ \sum_{k=1}^{n} \beta_{ik} p_k + \gamma_i y \right\}$

(s6) $\quad s_i = \alpha_i(\boldsymbol{q}) \exp\left\{ \sum_{k=1}^{n} \beta_{ik} p_k \right\} y^{\gamma_i}$

(s7) $\quad s_i = \alpha_i(\boldsymbol{q}) \prod_{k=1}^{n} p_k^{\beta_{ik}} \exp(\gamma_i y)$

(s8) $\quad s_i = \alpha_i(\boldsymbol{q}) \prod_{k=1}^{n} p_k^{\beta_{ik}} y^{\gamma_i}$

(x1) $\quad \beta_{ji} + \gamma_j x_i = \beta_{ij} + \gamma_i x_j$

(x2) $\quad \beta_{ji} + \dfrac{\gamma_j}{y} x_i = \beta_{ij} + \dfrac{\gamma_i}{y} x_j$

(x3) $\quad \dfrac{\beta_{ji}}{p_i} + \gamma_j x_i = \dfrac{\beta_{ij}}{p_j} + \gamma_i x_j$

(x4) $\quad \dfrac{\beta_{ji}}{p_i} + \dfrac{\gamma_j}{y} x_i = \dfrac{\beta_{ij}}{p_j} + \dfrac{\gamma_i}{y} x_j$

(x5) $\quad \beta_{ji} x_j + \gamma_j x_i x_j = \beta_{ij} x_i + \gamma_i x_i x_j$

(x6) $\quad \beta_{ji} x_j + \dfrac{\gamma_j}{y} x_i x_j = \beta_{ij} x_i + \dfrac{\gamma_i}{y} x_i x_j$

(x7) $\quad \dfrac{\beta_{ji}}{p_i} x_j + \gamma_j x_i x_j = \dfrac{\beta_{ij}}{p_j} x_i + \gamma_i x_i x_j$

(x8) $\quad \dfrac{\beta_{ji}}{p_i} x_j + \dfrac{\gamma_j}{y} x_i x_j = \dfrac{\beta_{ij}}{p_j} x_i + \dfrac{\gamma_i}{y} x_i x_j$

Table 5
Slutsky Symmetry Conditions for Incomplete Expenditure System Models

(e1) $\quad \dfrac{1}{p_i p_j}\left\{\beta_{ji} p_i + \gamma_j e_i\right\} = \dfrac{1}{p_i p_j}\left\{\beta_{ij} p_j + \gamma_i e_j\right\}$

(e2) $\quad \dfrac{1}{p_i p_j}\left\{\beta_{ji} p_i + \dfrac{\gamma_j}{y} e_i\right\} = \dfrac{1}{p_i p_j}\left\{\beta_{ij} p_j + \dfrac{\gamma_i}{y} e_j\right\}$

(e3) $\quad \dfrac{1}{p_i p_j}\left\{\beta_{ji} + \gamma_j e_i\right\} = \dfrac{1}{p_i p_j}\left\{\beta_{ij} + \gamma_i e_j\right\}$

(e4) $\quad \dfrac{1}{p_i p_j}\left\{\beta_{ji} + \dfrac{\gamma_j}{y} e_i\right\} = \dfrac{1}{p_i p_j}\left\{\beta_{ij} + \dfrac{\gamma_i}{y} e_j\right\}$

(e5) $\quad \dfrac{1}{p_i p_j}\left\{\beta_{ji} p_i e_j + \gamma_j e_i e_j\right\} = \dfrac{1}{p_i p_j}\left\{\beta_{ij} p_j e_i + \gamma_i e_i e_j\right\}$

(e6) $\quad \dfrac{1}{p_i p_j}\left\{\beta_{ji} p_i e_j + \dfrac{\gamma_j}{y} e_i e_j\right\} = \dfrac{1}{p_i p_j}\left\{\beta_{ij} p_j e_i + \dfrac{\gamma_i}{y} e_i e_j\right\}$

(e7) $\quad \dfrac{1}{p_i p_j}\left\{\beta_{ji} e_j + \gamma_j e_i e_j\right\} = \dfrac{1}{p_i p_j}\left\{\beta_{ij} e_i + \gamma_i e_i e_j\right\}$

(e8) $\quad \dfrac{1}{p_i p_j}\left\{\beta_{ji} e_j + \dfrac{\gamma_j}{y} e_i e_j\right\} = \dfrac{1}{p_i p_j}\left\{\beta_{ij} e_i + \dfrac{\gamma_i}{y} e_i e_j\right\}$

Table 6
Slutsky Symmetry Conditions for Incomplete Expenditure Share Models

(s1) $\quad \dfrac{y}{p_i p_j}\left\{\beta_{ji}p_i + (s_j + \gamma_j y)s_i\right\} = \dfrac{y}{p_i p_j}\left\{\beta_{ij}p_j + (s_i + \gamma_i y)s_j\right\}$

(s2) $\quad \dfrac{y}{p_i p_j}\left\{\beta_{ji}p_i + (s_j + \gamma_j)s_i\right\} = \dfrac{y}{p_i p_j}\left\{\beta_{ij}p_j + (s_i + \gamma_i)s_j\right\}$

(s3) $\quad \dfrac{y}{p_i p_j}\left\{\beta_{ji} + (s_j + \gamma_j y)s_i\right\} = \dfrac{y}{p_i p_j}\left\{\beta_{ij} + (s_i + \gamma_i y)s_j\right\}$

(s4) $\quad \dfrac{y}{p_i p_j}\left\{\beta_{ji} + (s_j + \gamma_j)s_i\right\} = \dfrac{y}{p_i p_j}\left\{\beta_{ij} + (s_i + \gamma_i)s_j\right\}$

(s5) $\quad \dfrac{y}{p_i p_j}\left\{\beta_{ji}p_i s_j + (1 + \gamma_j y)s_i s_j\right\} = \dfrac{y}{p_i p_j}\left\{\beta_{ij}p_j s_i + (1 + \gamma_i y)s_i s_j\right\}$

(s6) $\quad \dfrac{y}{p_i p_j}\left\{\beta_{ji}p_i s_j + (1 + \gamma_j)s_i s_j\right\} = \dfrac{y}{p_i p_j}\left\{\beta_{ij}p_j s_i + (1 + \gamma_i)s_i s_j\right\}$

(s7) $\quad \dfrac{y}{p_i p_j}\left\{\beta_{ji}s_j + (1 + \gamma_j y)s_i s_j\right\} = \dfrac{y}{p_i p_j}\left\{\beta_{ij}s_i + (1 + \gamma_i y)s_i s_j\right\}$

(s8) $\quad \dfrac{y}{p_i p_j}\left\{\beta_{ji}s_j + (1 + \gamma_j)s_i s_j\right\} = \dfrac{y}{p_i p_j}\left\{\beta_{ij}s_i + (1 + \gamma_i)s_i s_j\right\}$

Table 7
Slutsky Symmetry Restrictions for Incomplete Demand System Models

$(x1)^{1}$ 1a. $\beta_{ij} = \beta_{ji}, i, j \in N$

  1b. $\gamma_i = 0, i \in N$

  2a. $\alpha_i(q) = \dfrac{\gamma_i}{\gamma_1}\left\{\alpha_1(q) + \dfrac{\beta_{11}}{\gamma_1} - \dfrac{\beta_{1i}}{\gamma_i}\right\}, i \in J$

  2b. $\beta_{ij} = (\gamma_i/\gamma_1)\beta_{1j}, i \in J, j \in N$

2c. $\mathrm{sgn}(\gamma_i) = \mathrm{sgn}(\gamma_1) \neq 0, i \in J$

2d. $\beta_{ij} = 0, i \in N \sim J, j \in N$

2e. $\gamma_i = 0, i \in N \sim J$

2f. $\alpha_i(q) = -\beta_{1i}/\gamma_1 > 0, i \in N \sim J$

$(x2)$ 1a. $\beta_{ij} = \beta_{ji}, i, j \in N$

  1b. $\gamma_i = 0, i \in N$

2a. $\alpha_i(q) = (\gamma_i/\gamma_1)\alpha_1(q), i \in N$

2b. $\beta_{ij} = (\gamma_i\gamma_j/\gamma_1^2)\beta_{11}, i, j \in N$

2c. $\mathrm{sgn}(\gamma_i) = \mathrm{sgn}(\gamma_1) \neq 0, i \in N$

$(x3)$ 1a. $\beta_{ij} = 0, i, j \in N, i \neq j$
&
$(x4)$ 1b. $\gamma_i = 0, i \in N$

2a. $\beta_{ij} = 0, i, j \in N$

2b. $\alpha_i(q) = (\gamma_i/\gamma_1)\alpha_1(q), i \in N$

2c. $\mathrm{sgn}(\gamma_i) = \mathrm{sgn}(\gamma_1) \neq 0, i \in N$

$(x5)^{2,3}$ 1a. $\alpha_i(q) = (\beta_{ii}/\beta_{11})\alpha_1(q) > 0, i \in J$

  1b. $\gamma_i = \gamma_1, i \in K$

  1c. $\beta_{ij} = \beta_{jj}, i, j \in J$

1d. $\beta_{ij} = 0, i \in J, j \in K \sim J; i \in K \sim J,$
  $j \in K, i \neq j; i \in N \sim K, j \in N$

1e. $\gamma_i = 0, i \in N \sim K$

1f. $\alpha_i(q) = -\beta_{1i}/\gamma_1 > 0, i \in N \sim K$

$(x6)^{3}$ 1a. $\alpha_i(q) = (\beta_{ii}/\beta_{11})\alpha_1(q) > 0, i \in J$

  1b. $\gamma_i = \gamma_1, i \in N$

  1c. $\beta_{ij} = \beta_{jj}, i, j \in J$

  1d. $\beta_{ij} = 0, i \in J, j \in N \sim J;$
    $i \in N \sim J, j \in N, i \neq j$

  2a. $\alpha_i(q) = (\beta_{ii}/\beta_{11})\alpha_1(q) > 0, i \in J$

2b. $\gamma_i = \gamma_1, i \in K$

2c. $\beta_{ij} = \beta_{jj}, i, j \in J$

2d. $\beta_{ij} = 0, i \in J, j \in K \sim J; i \in K \sim J,$
  $j \in K, i \neq j; i \in N \sim K, j \in N$

2e. $\gamma_i = 1, i \in N \sim K$

2f. $\alpha_i(q) = \beta_{1i} > 0, i \in N \sim K$

$(x7)^{2,4}$

  1a. $\alpha_i(q) = \alpha_1(q)\left\{\dfrac{1+\beta_{ii}}{1+\beta_{11}}\right\} > 0, i \in J$

1e. $\beta_{ij} = 0, i \in J, j \in K \sim J; i \in K \sim J,$
  $j \in K, i \neq j; i \in N \sim K, j \in N, i \neq j$

  1b. $\beta_{ij} = 1 + \beta_{jj}, i, j \in J, i \neq j$

  1c. $\beta_{ij} = \beta_{1j}, i \in K, j \in N \sim K$

  1d. $\gamma_i = \gamma_1, i \in K$

1f. $\gamma_i = 0, i \in N \sim K$

1g. $\beta_{ii} = -1, i \in N \sim K$

1h. $\alpha_i(q) = -\beta_{1i}/\gamma_1 > 0, i \in N \sim K$

---

[1] LaFrance [1985] notes that an additional restriction arising from the negative semi-definiteness of the Slutsky matrix assumption is $\beta_{11} + \gamma_1 x_1 \leq 0$ for the J subset.

[2] Note that the $N{\sim}K$ subset is empty if $\gamma_1 = 0$.

[3] For the (x5-1) and (x6-2) restricted models, LaFrance [1990] further decomposes the $K{\sim}J$ subset into one set with $\beta_{kk} = 0$ and another with $\beta_{kk} \neq 0$. Similarly for the (x6-1) restricted model, LaFrance decomposes the $N{\sim}J$ subset into one set with $\beta_{kk} = 0$ and another with $\beta_{kk} \neq 0$.

$(x8)^4$

1a. $\alpha_i(q) = \alpha_1(q)\left\{\dfrac{1+\beta_{ii}}{1+\beta_{11}}\right\} > 0, i \in J$

1b. $\beta_{ij} = 1 + \beta_{jj}, \; i, j \in J, i \neq j$

1c. $\gamma_i = \gamma_1, i \in N$

1d. $\beta_{ij} = 0, i \in J, j \in N \sim J;$

$\quad i \in N \sim J, j \in N, i \neq j$

2a. $\alpha_i(q) = \alpha_1(q)\left\{\dfrac{1+\beta_{ii}}{1+\beta_{11}}\right\} > 0, i \in J$

2b. $\beta_{ij} = 1 + \beta_{jj}, i, j \in J, i \neq j$

2c. $\alpha_i(q) = \beta_{1i} > 0, i \in N \sim K$

2d. $\gamma_i = 0, i \in K$

2e. $\gamma_i = 1, i \in N \sim K$

2f. $\beta_{ij} = \beta_{1j}, \; i \in K, j \in N \sim K$

2g. $\beta_{ii} = -1, i \in N \sim K$

2h. $\beta_{ij} = 0, i \in J, j \in K \sim J;$

$\quad i \in K \sim J, j \in K, i \neq j;$

$\quad i \in N \sim K, j \in N, i \neq j$

---

[4] For the (x7-1) and (x8-2) restricted models, LaFrance [1990] further decomposes the $K \sim J$ subset into one set with $\beta_{kk} = -1$ and another with $\beta_{kk} \neq -1$. Similarly for the (x8-1) restricted model, LaFrance decomposes the $N \sim J$ subset into one set with $\beta_{kk} = -1$ and another with $\beta_{kk} \neq -1$.

Table 8
Slutsky Symmetry Restrictions for Incomplete Expenditure System Models

(e1)   1a. $\beta_{ij} = 0, i, j \in N, i \neq j$

1b. $\gamma_i = 0, i \in N$

2a. $\gamma_i = 1, i \in J$

2b. $\beta_{ii} = 0, i \in J$

2c. $\alpha_i(q) = (\gamma_i / \gamma_1)\alpha_1(q), i \in K$

2d. $\gamma_i \neq 0, 1, i \in K \sim J$

2e. $\beta_{ij} = \gamma_i \beta_{jj} / (\gamma_j - 1), i \in K, j \in K \sim J$

2f. $\beta_{ik} = (\gamma_i / \gamma_j)\beta_{jk}, i, j \in K, k \in N,$
      $k \neq i, j$

2g. $\beta_{ij} = 0, i \in N \sim K, j \in N, i \neq j$

2h. $\gamma_i = 0, i \in N \sim K$

2i. $\alpha_i(q) = 0, i \in N \sim K$

2j. $\beta_{ii} = -\beta_{1i} / \gamma_1 > 0, i \in N \sim K$

3a. $\gamma_1 = 1$

3b. $\gamma_i = 0, i \in N, i \neq 1$

3c. $\beta_{ij} = 0, i, j \in N, i \neq 1, j \neq i, 1$

3d. $\beta_{ii} = -\beta_{1i}, i \in N, i \neq 1$

3e. $\alpha_i(q) = 0, i \in N, i \neq 1$

(e2)   1a. $\beta_{ij} = 0, i, j \in N, i \neq j$

1b. $\gamma_i = 0, i \in N$

2a. $\beta_{ij} = 0, i, j \in N$

2b. $\alpha_i(q) = (\gamma_i / \gamma_1)\alpha_1(q), i \in N$

2c. $\mathrm{sgn}(\gamma_i) = \mathrm{sgn}(\gamma_1) \neq 0, i \in N$

(e3)   1a. $\beta_{ij} = \beta_{ji}, i, j \in N$

1b. $\gamma_i = 0, i \in N$

2a. $\beta_{ij} = (\gamma_i / \gamma_1)\beta_{1j}, i, j \in J$

2b. $\beta_{ij} = 0, i \in N \sim J, j \in N$

2c. $\mathrm{sgn}(\gamma_i) \neq 0, i \in J$

2d. $\gamma_i = 0, i \in N \sim J$

2e. $\alpha_i(q) = \dfrac{\gamma_i}{\gamma_1}\left\{\alpha_1(q) - \dfrac{\beta_{1i}}{\gamma_i} + \dfrac{\beta_{i1}}{\gamma_i}\right\}, i \in J$

2f. $\alpha_i(q) = -\beta_{1i} / \gamma_1 > 0, i \in N \sim J$

(e4)   1a. $\beta_{ij} = \beta_{ji}, i, j \in N$

1b. $\gamma_i = 0, i \in N$

2a. $\alpha_i(q) = (\gamma_i / \gamma_1)\alpha_1(q), i \in N$

2b. $\beta_{ij} = (\gamma_i \gamma_j / \gamma_1^2)\beta_{11}, i, j \in N$

2c. $\mathrm{sgn}(\gamma_i) = \mathrm{sgn}(\gamma_1) \neq 0, i \in N$

(e5)   1a. $\beta_{ij} = 0, i, j \in N, i \neq j$ 1b. $\gamma_i = \gamma_1, i \in N$

(e6)   1a. $\beta_{ij} = 0, i, j \in N, i \neq j$ 1b. $\gamma_i = \gamma_1, i \in N$

(e7)[1]   1a. $\alpha_i(q) = (\beta_{ii} / \beta_{11})\alpha_1(q) > 0, i \in J$

1b. $\beta_{ij} = \beta_{jj}, i, j \in J$

1c. $\beta_{ij} = \beta_{1j}, i \in K, j \in N \sim K$

1d. $\gamma_i = \gamma_1, i \in K$

1e. $\beta_{ij} = 0, i \in J, j \in K \sim J; i \in K \sim J,$
      $j \in K, i \neq j; i \in N \sim K, j \in N$

1f. $\gamma_i = 0, i \in N \sim K$

1g. $\alpha_i(q) = -\beta_{1i} / \gamma_1 > 0, i \in N \sim K$

---

[1] Note that the $N{\sim}K$ subset is empty if $\gamma_1 = 0$.

Table 8 (cont.)
Slutsky Symmetry Restrictions for Incomplete Expenditure System Models

(e8)
1a. $\alpha_i(\boldsymbol{q}) = (\beta_{ii} / \beta_{11})\alpha_1(\boldsymbol{q}) > 0, i \in J$

1b. $\beta_{ij} = \beta_{jj}, \; i, j \in J$

1c. $\gamma_i = \gamma_1, i \in N$

1d. $\beta_{ij} = 0, i \in J, j \in N \sim J;$

  $\quad i \in N \sim J, j \in N, i \neq j$

2a. $\alpha_i(\boldsymbol{q}) = (\beta_{ii} / \beta_{11})\alpha_1(\boldsymbol{q}) > 0, i \in J$

2b. $\beta_{ij} = \beta_{jj}, i, j \in J$

2c. $\alpha_i(\boldsymbol{q}) = \beta_{1i} > 0, i \in N \sim K$

2d. $\gamma_i = 0, i \in K$

2e. $\gamma_i = 1, i \in N \sim K$

2f. $\beta_{ij} = \beta_{1j}, \; i \in K, j \in N \sim K$

2g. $\beta_{ij} = 0, i \in J, j \in K \sim J;$

  $\quad i \in K \sim J, j \in K, i \neq j;$

  $\quad i \in N \sim K, j \in N$

(s1) 1a. $\gamma_i = 0, i \in N$ 2b. $\beta_{ij} = 0, i, j \in N$

1b. $\beta_{ij} = 0, i, j \in N, i \neq j$ 2c. $\text{sgn}(\gamma_i) = \text{sgn}(\gamma_1) \neq 0, i \in N$

2a. $\alpha_i(\boldsymbol{q}) = (\gamma_i / \gamma_1)\alpha_1(\boldsymbol{q}),\ i \in N$

(s2) 1a. $\gamma_i = 0, i \in N$ 2g. $\beta_{ik} = (\gamma_i / \gamma_j)\beta_{jk}, i, j \in K, k \in N,$

1b. $\beta_{ij} = 0, i, j \in N, i \neq j$ $k \neq i, j$

2a. $\gamma_i = 1, i \in J$ 2h. $\beta_{ij} = 0, i \in N \sim K, j \in N, i \neq j$

2b. $\gamma_i \neq 0, 1, i \in K \sim J$ 2i. $\alpha_i(\boldsymbol{q}) = 0, i \in N \sim K$

2c. $\gamma_i = 0, i \in N \sim K$ 2j. $\beta_{ii} = -\beta_{1i} / \gamma_1 > 0, i \in N \sim K$

2d. $\alpha_i(\boldsymbol{q}) = (\gamma_i / \gamma_1)\alpha_1(\boldsymbol{q}), i \in K$ 3a. $\gamma_1 = 1$

2e. $\beta_{ii} = 0, i \in J$ 3b. $\gamma_i = 0, i \in N, i \neq 1$

3c. $\beta_{ij} = 0, i, j \in N, i \neq 1, j \neq i, 1$

2f. $\beta_{ij} = \dfrac{\gamma_i \beta_{jj}}{\gamma_j - 1}, i \in K, j \in K \sim J, i \neq j$ 3d. $\beta_{ii} = -\beta_{1i}, i \in N, i \neq 1$

3e. $\alpha_i(\boldsymbol{q}) = 0, i \in N, i \neq 1$

(s3) 1a. $\beta_{ij} = \beta_{ji}, i, j \in N$ 2b. $\beta_{ij} = (\gamma_i \gamma_j / \gamma_1^2)\beta_{11}, i, j \in N$

1b. $\gamma_i = 0, i \in N$ 2c. $\text{sgn}(\gamma_i) = \text{sgn}(\gamma_1) \neq 0, i \in N$

2a. $\alpha_i(\boldsymbol{q}) = (\gamma_i / \gamma_1)\alpha_1(\boldsymbol{q}), i \in N$

(s4) 1a. $\beta_{ij} = \beta_{ji}, i, j \in N$ 2b. $\beta_{ij} = (\gamma_i / \gamma_1)\beta_{1j}, i \in J, j \in N$

1b. $\gamma_i = 0, i \in N$ 2c. $\alpha_i(\boldsymbol{q}) = -\beta_{1i} / \gamma_1 > 0, i \in N \sim J$

2d. $\beta_{ij} = 0, i \in N \sim J, j \in N$

2a. $\alpha_i(\boldsymbol{q}) = \dfrac{\gamma_i}{\gamma_1}\left\{\dfrac{\beta_{i1}}{\gamma_i} - \dfrac{\beta_{1i}}{\gamma_i} + \alpha_1(\boldsymbol{q})\right\}, i \in J$ 2e. $\gamma_i = 0, i \in N \sim J$

2f. $\text{sgn}(\gamma_i) \neq 0, i \in J$

(s5) 1a. $\beta_{ij} = 0, i, j \in N, i \neq j$ 1b. $\gamma_i = \gamma_1, i \in N$

(s6) 1a. $\beta_{ij} = 0, i, j \in N, i \neq j$ 1b. $\gamma_i = \gamma_1, i \in N$

(s7) 1a. $\alpha_i(\boldsymbol{q}) = (\beta_{ii} / \beta_{11})\alpha_1(\boldsymbol{q}) > 0, i \in J$ 1d. $\beta_{ij} = 0, i \in J, j \in N \sim J;$

1b. $\beta_{ij} = \beta_{jj},\ i, j \in J$ $i \in N \sim J, j \in N, i \neq j$

1c. $\gamma_i = \gamma_1, i \in N$

Table 9 (cont.)
Slutsky Symmetry Restrictions for Incomplete Expenditure Share System Models

(s8)

1a. $\alpha_i(\boldsymbol{q}) = (\beta_{ii} / \beta_{11})\alpha_1(\boldsymbol{q}) > 0, i \in J$

1b. $\beta_{ij} = \beta_{jj}, \ i, j \in J$

1c. $\gamma_i = \gamma_1, i \in N$

1d. $\beta_{ij} = 0, i \in J, j \in N \sim J;$

   $i \in N \sim J, j \in N, i \neq j$

2a. $\alpha_i(\boldsymbol{q}) = (\beta_{ii} / \beta_{11})\alpha_1(\boldsymbol{q}) > 0, i \in J$

2b. $\beta_{ij} = \beta_{jj}, \ i, j \in J$

2c. $\alpha_i(\boldsymbol{q}) = \beta_{1i} > 0, i \in N \sim K$

2d. $\gamma_i = -1, i \in K$

2e. $\gamma_i = 0, i \in N \sim K$

2f. $\beta_{ij} = \beta_{1j}, i \in K, j \in N \sim K$

2g. $\beta_{ij} = 0, i \in J, j \in K \sim J;$

   $i \in K \sim J, j \in K, i \neq j;$

   $i \in N \sim K, j \in N$

Table 10
Restricted Incomplete Demand System Models

(x1) 1. $x_i = \alpha_i(\boldsymbol{q}) + \sum_{k \in N} \beta_{ik} p_k, i \in N$

 2. $x_i = \dfrac{\gamma_i}{\gamma_1}\left\{\alpha_1(\boldsymbol{q}) + \dfrac{\beta_{11}}{\gamma_1} - \dfrac{\beta_{1i}}{\gamma_i} + \sum_{k \in N} \beta_{1k} p_k + \gamma_1 y\right\}, i \in J$

 $x_i = -\beta_{1i}/\gamma_1, i \in N \sim J$

(x2) 1. $x_i = \alpha_i(\boldsymbol{q}) + \sum_{k \in N} \beta_{ik} p_k, i \in N$

 2. $x_i = \dfrac{\gamma_i}{\gamma_1}\left\{\alpha_1(\boldsymbol{q}) + \dfrac{\beta_{11}}{\gamma_1} \sum_{k \in N} \gamma_k p_k + \gamma_1 \ln y\right\}, i \in N$

(x3) 1. $x_i = \alpha_i(\boldsymbol{q}) + \beta_{ii} \ln p_i, i \in N$

 2. $x_i = (\gamma_i / \gamma_1)(\alpha_1(\boldsymbol{q}) + \gamma_1 y), i \in N$

(x4) 1. $x_i = \alpha_i(\boldsymbol{q}) + \beta_{ii} \ln p_i, i \in N$

 2. $x_i = (\gamma_i / \gamma_1)(\alpha_1(\boldsymbol{q}) + \gamma_1 \ln y), i \in N$

(x5) 1.[1] $x_i = \dfrac{\beta_{ii}}{\beta_{11}} \alpha_1(\boldsymbol{q}) \exp\left\{\sum_{k \in J} \beta_{kk} p_k + \sum_{k \in N \sim K} \beta_{1k} p_k + \gamma_1 y\right\}, i \in J$

 $x_i = \alpha_i(\boldsymbol{q}) \exp\left\{\beta_{ii} p_i + \sum_{k \in N \sim K} \beta_{1k} p_k + \gamma_1 y\right\}, i \in K \sim J$

 $x_i = -\beta_{1i}/\gamma_1, i \in N \sim K$

(x6) 1. $x_i = \dfrac{\beta_{ii}}{\beta_{11}} \alpha_1(\boldsymbol{q}) \exp\left\{\sum_{k \in J} \beta_{kk} p_k\right\} y^{\gamma_1}, i \in J$

 $x_i = \alpha_i(\boldsymbol{q}) \exp(\beta_{ii} p_i) y^{\gamma_1}, i \in N \sim J$

 2. $x_i = \dfrac{\beta_{ii}}{\beta_{11}} \alpha_1(\boldsymbol{q}) \exp\left\{\sum_{k \in J} \beta_{kk} p_k + \sum_{k \in N \sim K} \beta_{1k} p_k\right\}, i \in J$

 $x_i = \alpha_i(\boldsymbol{q}) \exp\left\{\beta_{ii} p_i + \sum_{k \in N \sim K} \beta_{1k} p_k\right\}, i \in K \sim J$

 $x_i = \beta_{1i} y, i \in N \sim K$

(x7) 1.[1] $x_i = \alpha_1(\boldsymbol{q})\left\{\dfrac{1+\beta_{ii}}{1+\beta_{11}}\right\} p_i^{-1} \prod_{k \in J} p_k^{1+\beta_{kk}} \prod_{k \in N \sim K} p_k^{\beta_{1k}} \exp(\gamma_1 y), i \in J$

 $x_i = \alpha_i(\boldsymbol{q}) p_i^{\beta_{ii}} \prod_{k \in N \sim K} p_k^{\beta_{1k}} \exp(\gamma_1 y), i \in K \sim J$

 $x_i = -(\beta_{1i}/\gamma_1) p_i^{-1}, i \in N \sim K$

---

[1] Note that the $N \sim K$ subset is empty if $\gamma_1 = 0$.

Table 10 (cont.)
Restricted Incomplete Demand System Models

(x8) 1.

$$x_i = \alpha_1(\boldsymbol{q})\left\{\frac{1+\beta_{ii}}{1+\beta_{11}}\right\}p_i^{-1}\prod_{k\in J}p_k^{1+\beta_{kk}}y^{\gamma_1}, i\in J$$

$$x_i = \alpha_i(\boldsymbol{q})p_i^{\beta_{ii}}y^{\gamma_1}, i\in N\sim J$$

2.

$$x_i = \alpha_1(\boldsymbol{q})\left\{\frac{1+\beta_{ii}}{1+\beta_{11}}\right\}p_i^{-1}\prod_{k\in J}p_k^{1+\beta_{kk}}\prod_{k\in N\sim K}p_k^{\beta_{1k}}, i\in J$$

$$x_i = \alpha_i(\boldsymbol{q})p_i^{\beta_{ii}}\prod_{k\in N\sim K}p_k^{\beta_{1k}}, i\in K\sim J$$

$$x_i = \beta_{1i}p_i^{-1}y, i\in N\sim K$$

Table 11
Restricted Incomplete Expenditure System Models

(e1) 1. $e_i = \alpha_i(\boldsymbol{q}) + \beta_{ii} p_i, i \in N$

 2. $e_i = \alpha_1(\boldsymbol{q}) + \sum_{k \in K, i \neq k} \beta_{ik} p_k + \sum_{k \in N \sim K} \beta_{1k} p_k + y, i \in J$

 $e_i = \dfrac{\gamma_i}{\gamma_1} \alpha_1(\boldsymbol{q}) + \sum_{k \in K} \beta_{ik} p_k + \dfrac{\gamma_i}{\gamma_1} \sum_{k \in N \sim K} \beta_{1k} p_k + \gamma_i y, i \in K \sim J$

 $e_i = -(\beta_{1i} / \gamma_1) p_i, i \in N \sim K$

 3. $e_1 = \alpha_1(\boldsymbol{q}) + \sum_{k \in N} \beta_{1k} p_k + y$

 $e_i = \beta_{i1} p_1 - \beta_{1i} p_i, i \in N, i \neq 1$

(e2) 1. $e_i = \alpha_i(\boldsymbol{q}) + \beta_{ii} p_i, i \in N$

 2. $e_i = (\gamma_i / \gamma_1)(\alpha_1(\boldsymbol{q}) + \gamma_1 \ln y), i \in N$

(e3) 1. $e_i = \alpha_i(\boldsymbol{q}) + \sum_{k \in N} \beta_{ik} \ln p_k, i \in N$

 2. $e_i = \dfrac{\gamma_i}{\gamma_1} \left\{ \alpha_1(\boldsymbol{q}) - \dfrac{\beta_{1i}}{\gamma_i} + \dfrac{\beta_{i1}}{\gamma_i} + \sum_{k \in N} \beta_{1k} \ln p_k + \gamma_1 y \right\}, i \in J$

 $e_i = -\beta_{1i} / \gamma_1, i \in N \sim J$

(e4) 1. $e_i = \alpha_i(\boldsymbol{q}) + \sum_{k \in N} \beta_{ik} \ln p_k, i \in N$

 2. $e_i = \dfrac{\gamma_i}{\gamma_1} \left\{ \alpha_1(\boldsymbol{q}) + \dfrac{\beta_{11}}{\gamma_1} \sum_{k \in N} \gamma_k \ln p_k + \gamma_1 \ln y \right\}, i \in N$

(e5) 1. $e_i = \alpha_i(\boldsymbol{q}) \exp(\beta_{ii} p_i + \gamma_1 y), i \in N$

(e6) 1. $e_i = \alpha_i(\boldsymbol{q}) \exp(\beta_{ii} p_i) y^{\gamma_1}, i \in N$

(e7)[1] 1. $e_i = (\beta_{ii} / \beta_{11}) \alpha_1(\boldsymbol{q}) \prod_{k \in J} p_k^{\beta_{kk}} \prod_{k \in N \sim K} p_k^{\beta_{1k}} \exp(\gamma_1 y), i \in J$

 $e_i = \alpha_i(\boldsymbol{q}) p_i^{\beta_{ii}} \prod_{k \in N \sim K} p_k^{\beta_{1k}} \exp(\gamma_1 y), i \in K \sim J$

 $e_i = -(\beta_{1i} / \gamma_1), i \in N \sim K$

(e8) 1. $e_i = (\beta_{ii} / \beta_{11}) \alpha_1(\boldsymbol{q}) \prod_{k \in J} p_k^{\beta_{kk}} y^{\gamma_1}, i \in J$

 $e_i = \alpha_i(\boldsymbol{q}) p_i^{\beta_{ii}} y^{\gamma_1}, i \in N \sim J$

 2. $e_i = (\beta_{ii} / \beta_{11}) \alpha_1(\boldsymbol{q}) \prod_{k \in J} p_k^{\beta_{kk}} \prod_{k \in N \sim K} p_k^{\beta_{1k}}, i \in J$

 $e_i = \alpha_i(\boldsymbol{q}) p_i^{\beta_{ii}} \prod_{k \in N \sim K} p_k^{\beta_{1k}}, i \in K \sim J$

 $e_i = \beta_{1i} y, i \in N \sim K$

---

[1] Note that the $N{\sim}K$ subset is empty if $\gamma_1 = 0$.

Table 12
Restricted Incomplete Expenditure Share System Models

(s1)   1. $s_i = \alpha_i(\boldsymbol{q}) + \beta_{ii} p_i, i \in N$

        2. $s_i = (\gamma_i / \gamma_1)(\alpha_1(\boldsymbol{q}) + \gamma_1 y), i \in N$

(s2)   1. $s_i = \alpha_i(\boldsymbol{q}) + \beta_{ii} p_i, i \in N$

        2. $s_i = \alpha_1(\boldsymbol{q}) + \sum_{k \in K, i \neq k} \beta_{ik} p_k + \sum_{k \in N \sim K} \beta_{1k} p_k + \ln y, i \in J$

$$s_i = \frac{\gamma_i}{\gamma_1} \alpha_1(\boldsymbol{q}) + \sum_{k \in K} \beta_{ik} p_k + \frac{\gamma_i}{\gamma_1} \sum_{k \in N \sim K} \beta_{1k} p_k + \gamma_i \ln y, i \in K \sim J$$

$$s_i = -(\beta_{1i} / \gamma_1) p_i, i \in N \sim K$$

        3. $s_1 = \alpha_1(\boldsymbol{q}) + \sum_{k \in N} \beta_{1k} p_k + \ln y$

$$s_i = \beta_{i1} p_1 - \beta_{1i} p_i, i \in N, i \neq 1$$

(s3)   1. $s_i = \alpha_i(\boldsymbol{q}) + \sum_{k \in N} \beta_{ik} \ln p_k, i \in N$

        2. $s_i = \frac{\gamma_i}{\gamma_1} \left\{ \alpha_1(\boldsymbol{q}) + \frac{\beta_{11}}{\gamma_1} \sum_{k \in N} \gamma_K \ln p_k + \gamma_1 y \right\}, i \in N$

(s4)   1. $s_i = \alpha_i(\boldsymbol{q}) + \sum_{k \in N} \beta_{ik} \ln p_k, i \in N$

        2. $s_i = \frac{\gamma_i}{\gamma_1} \left\{ \frac{\beta_{i1}}{\gamma_i} - \frac{\beta_{1i}}{\gamma_i} + \alpha_1(\boldsymbol{q}) + \sum_{k \in N} \beta_{1k} \ln p_k + \gamma_1 \ln y \right\}, i \in J$

$$s_i = -\beta_{1i} / \gamma_1, i \in N \sim J$$

(s5)   1. $s_i = \alpha_i(\boldsymbol{q}) \exp(\beta_{ii} p_i + \gamma_1 y), i \in N$

(s6)   1. $s_i = \alpha_i(\boldsymbol{q}) \exp(\beta_{ii} p_i) y^{\gamma_1}, i \in N$

(s7)   1. $s_i = (\beta_{ii} / \beta_{11}) \alpha_1(\boldsymbol{q}) \prod_{k \in J} p_k^{\beta_{kk}} \exp(\gamma_1 y), i \in J$

$$s_i = \alpha_i(\boldsymbol{q}) p_i^{\beta_{ii}} \exp(\gamma_1 y), i \in N \sim J$$

(s8)   1. $s_i = (\beta_{ii} / \beta_{11}) \alpha_1(\boldsymbol{q}) \prod_{k \in J} p_k^{\beta_{kk}} y^{\gamma_1}, i \in J$

$$s_i = \alpha_i(\boldsymbol{q}) p_i^{\beta_{ii}} y^{\gamma_1}, i \in N \sim J$$

        2. $s_i = (\beta_{ii} / \beta_{11}) \alpha_1(\boldsymbol{q}) \prod_{k \in J} p_k^{\beta_{kk}} \prod_{k \in N \sim K} p_k^{\beta_{1k}} y^{-1}, i \in J$

$$s_i = \alpha_i(\boldsymbol{q}) p_i^{\beta_{ii}} \prod_{k \in N \sim K} p_k^{\beta_{1k}} y^{-1}, i \in K \sim J$$

$$s_i = \beta_{1i}, i \in N \sim K$$

Table 13
Quasi-Indirect Utility Functions for Incomplete Demand System Models[1]

Model	Restrictions	Quasi-Indirect Utility Function
(x1)-1 & (x2)-1		$\phi(\boldsymbol{p},\boldsymbol{q},y) = y - \sum_{k\in N}\alpha_k(\boldsymbol{q})p_k - \frac{1}{2}\sum_{k\in N}\sum_{j\in N}\beta_{kj}p_k p_j$
(x1)-2		$\phi(\boldsymbol{p},\boldsymbol{q},y) = \left\{y + \frac{1}{\gamma_1}\left[\sum_{k\in N}\beta_{1k}p_k + \alpha_1(\boldsymbol{q}) + \frac{\beta_{11}}{\gamma_1}\right]\right\}\exp\left\{-\sum_{k\in J}\gamma_k p_k\right\}$
(x3)-1 & (x4)-1		$\phi(\boldsymbol{p},\boldsymbol{q},y) = y - \sum_{k\in N}\alpha_k(\boldsymbol{q})p_k - \sum_{k\in N}\beta_{kk}p_k(\ln p_k -1)$
(x3)-2		$\phi(\boldsymbol{p},\boldsymbol{q},y) = \left\{y + \frac{\alpha_1(\boldsymbol{q})}{\gamma_1}\right\}\left\{\exp\left[-\sum_{k\in N}\gamma_k p_k\right]\right\}$
(x5)-1	$\gamma_1 = 0$ $N\sim K = 0$	$\phi(\boldsymbol{p},\boldsymbol{q},y) = y - \frac{\alpha_1(\boldsymbol{q})}{\beta_{11}}\exp\left\{\sum_{k\in J}\beta_{kk}p_k\right\} - \sum_{\substack{k\in N\sim J \\ \beta_{kk}\neq 0}}\frac{\alpha_k(\boldsymbol{q})}{\beta_{kk}}\exp(\beta_{kk}p_k) - \sum_{\substack{k\in K\sim J \\ \beta_{kk}=0}}\alpha_k(\boldsymbol{q})p_k$
(x5)-1	$\gamma_1 \neq 0$	$\phi(\boldsymbol{p},\boldsymbol{q},y) = \frac{-\exp(-\gamma_1 y)}{\gamma_1}\exp\left\{-\sum_{k\in N\sim K}\beta_{1k}p_k - \sum_{\substack{k\in N\sim J \\ \beta_{kk}\neq 0}}\frac{\alpha_1(\boldsymbol{q})}{\beta_{11}}\exp\left[\sum_{k\in J}\beta_{kk}p_k\right] - \sum_{\substack{k\in N\sim J \\ \beta_{kk}\neq 0}}\frac{\alpha_k(\boldsymbol{q})}{\beta_{kk}}\exp(\beta_{kk}p_k) - \sum_{\substack{k\in K\sim J \\ \beta_{kk}=0}}\alpha_k(\boldsymbol{q})p_k\right\}$
(x6)-1	$\gamma_1 = 0$	$\phi(\boldsymbol{p},\boldsymbol{q},y) = y - \frac{\alpha_1(\boldsymbol{q})}{\beta_{11}}\exp\left\{\sum_{k\in J}\beta_{kk}p_k\right\} - \sum_{\substack{k\in N\sim J \\ \beta_{kk}\neq 0}}\frac{\alpha_k(\boldsymbol{q})}{\beta_{kk}}\exp(\beta_{kk}p_k) - \sum_{\substack{k\in N\sim J \\ \beta_{kk}=0}}\alpha_k(\boldsymbol{q})p_k$
(x6)-1	$\gamma_1 = 1$	$\phi(\boldsymbol{p},\boldsymbol{q},y) = \ln y - \frac{\alpha_1(\boldsymbol{q})}{\beta_{11}}\exp\left\{\sum_{k\in J}\beta_{kk}p_k\right\} - \sum_{\substack{k\in N\sim J \\ \beta_{kk}\neq 0}}\frac{\alpha_k(\boldsymbol{q})}{\beta_{kk}}\exp(\beta_{kk}p_k) - \sum_{\substack{k\in N\sim J \\ \beta_{kk}=0}}\alpha_k(\boldsymbol{q})p_{kk}$

Table 13 (cont.)
Quasi-Indirect Utility Functions for Incomplete Demand System Models

Model	Restrictions	Quasi-Indirect Utility Function
(x6)-1	$\gamma_1\neq 1,0$	$\phi(\boldsymbol{p},\boldsymbol{q},y)=\dfrac{y^{1-\gamma_1}}{1-\gamma_1}-\dfrac{\alpha_1(\boldsymbol{q})}{\beta_{11}}\exp\left\{\sum\limits_{k\in J}\beta_{kk}p_k\right\}-\sum\limits_{\substack{k\in N\sim J\\ \beta_{kk}\neq 0}}\dfrac{\alpha_k(\boldsymbol{q})}{\beta_{kk}}\exp(\beta_{kk}p_k)-\sum\limits_{\substack{k\in N\sim J\\ \beta_{kk}=0}}\alpha_k(\boldsymbol{q})p_k$
(x6)-2		$\phi(\boldsymbol{p},\boldsymbol{q},y)=y\exp\left\{-\dfrac{\alpha_1(\boldsymbol{q})}{\beta_{11}}\exp\left\{\sum\limits_{k\in J}\beta_{kk}p_k\right\}-\sum\limits_{\substack{k\in K\sim J\\ \beta_{kk}\neq 0}}\dfrac{\alpha_k(\boldsymbol{q})}{\beta_{kk}}\exp(\beta_{kk}p_k)-\sum\limits_{\substack{k\in K\sim J\\ \beta_{kk}=0}}\alpha_k(\boldsymbol{q})p_k\right\}$
(x7)-1	$\gamma_1=0$ & $N\sim K=0$	$\phi(\boldsymbol{p},\boldsymbol{q},y)=y-\dfrac{\alpha_1(\boldsymbol{q})}{1+\beta_{11}}\prod\limits_{k\in J}p_k^{1+\beta_{kk}}-\sum\limits_{k\in K\sim J}\dfrac{\alpha_k(\boldsymbol{q})}{1+\beta_{kk}}p_k^{1+\beta_{kk}}-\sum\limits_{k\in N\sim K}\alpha_k(\boldsymbol{q})\ln p_k$
(x7)-1	$\gamma_1\neq 0$	$\phi(\boldsymbol{p},\boldsymbol{q},y)=\dfrac{-\exp(-\gamma_1 y)}{\gamma_1}-\dfrac{\alpha_1(\boldsymbol{q})}{1+\beta_{11}}\prod\limits_{k\in J}p_k^{1+\beta_{kk}}-\sum\limits_{\substack{k\in N\sim J\\ \beta_{kk}\neq -1}}\dfrac{\alpha_k(\boldsymbol{q})}{1+\beta_{kk}}p_k^{1+\beta_{kk}}-\sum\limits_{\substack{k\in K\sim J\\ \beta_{kk}=-1}}\alpha_k(\boldsymbol{q})\ln p_k$
(x8)-1	$\gamma_1=1$	$\phi(\boldsymbol{p},\boldsymbol{q},y)=\ln y-\dfrac{\alpha_1(\boldsymbol{q})}{1+\beta_{11}}\prod\limits_{k\in J}p_k^{1+\beta_{kk}}-\sum\limits_{\substack{k\in N\sim J\\ \beta_{kk}\neq -1}}\dfrac{\alpha_k(\boldsymbol{q})}{1+\beta_{kk}}p_k^{1+\beta_{kk}}-\sum\limits_{\substack{k\in N\sim J\\ \beta_{kk}=-1}}\alpha_k(\boldsymbol{q})\ln p_k$
(x8)-1	$\gamma_1\neq 1$	$\phi(\boldsymbol{p},\boldsymbol{q},y)=\dfrac{y^{1-\gamma_1}}{1-\gamma_1}-\dfrac{\alpha_1(\boldsymbol{q})}{1+\beta_{11}}\prod\limits_{k\in J}p_k^{1+\beta_{kk}}-\sum\limits_{\substack{k\in N\sim J\\ \beta_{kk}\neq -1}}\dfrac{\alpha_k(\boldsymbol{q})}{1+\beta_{kk}}p_k^{1+\beta_{kk}}-\sum\limits_{\substack{k\in N\sim J\\ \beta_{kk}=-1}}\alpha_k(\boldsymbol{q})\ln p_k$
(x8)-2		$\phi(\boldsymbol{p},\boldsymbol{q},y)=y\prod\limits_{k\in N\sim K}p_k^{-\beta_{kk}}-\dfrac{\alpha_1(\boldsymbol{q})}{1+\beta_{11}}\prod\limits_{k\in J}p_k^{1+\beta_{kk}}-\sum\limits_{\substack{k\in N\sim J\\ \beta_{kk}\neq -1}}\dfrac{\alpha_k(\boldsymbol{q})}{1+\beta_{kk}}p_k^{1+\beta_{kk}}-\sum\limits_{\substack{k\in K\sim J\\ \beta_{kk}=-1}}\alpha_k(\boldsymbol{q})\ln p_k$

---

[1] The results reported here correct for typographical errors found in LaFrance [1990].

Table 14
Quasi-Indirect Utility Functions for Restricted Incomplete Expenditure System Models

Model	Restrictions	Quasi-Indirect Utility Function
(e1)-1 & (e2)-1		$\phi(\boldsymbol{p},\boldsymbol{q},y) = y - \sum_{k\in N}\alpha_k(\boldsymbol{q})\ln p_k - \sum_{k\in N}\beta_{kk}p_k$
(e3)-1 & (e4)-1		$\phi(\boldsymbol{p},\boldsymbol{q},y) = y - \sum_{k\in N}\alpha_k(\boldsymbol{q})\ln p_k - \tfrac{1}{2}\sum_{k\in N}\sum_{j\in N}\beta_{kj}\ln p_k \ln p_j$
(e7)-1	$\gamma_1 = 0$ $N\sim K = 0$	$\phi(\boldsymbol{p},\boldsymbol{q},y) = y - \dfrac{\alpha_1(\boldsymbol{q})}{\beta_{11}}\prod_{k\in J}p_k^{\beta_{kk}} - \sum_{\substack{k\in K\sim J\\ \beta_{kk}\neq 0}}\dfrac{\alpha_k(\boldsymbol{q})}{\beta_{kk}}p_k^{\beta_{kk}} - \sum_{\substack{k\in K\sim J\\ \beta_{kk}=0}}\alpha_k(\boldsymbol{q})\ln p_k$
(e7)-1	$\gamma_1 \neq 0$	$\phi(\boldsymbol{p},\boldsymbol{q},y) = \dfrac{-\exp(-\gamma_1 y)}{\gamma_1}\prod_{k\in N\sim K}p_k^{-\beta_{kk}} - \dfrac{\alpha_1(\boldsymbol{q})}{\beta_{11}}\prod_{k\in J}p_k^{\beta_{kk}} - \sum_{\substack{k\in N\sim J\\ \beta_{kk}\neq 0}}\dfrac{\alpha_k(\boldsymbol{q})}{\beta_{kk}}p_k^{\beta_{kk}} - \sum_{\substack{k\in K\sim J\\ \beta_{kk}=0}}\alpha_k(\boldsymbol{q})\ln p_k$
(e8)-1	$\gamma_1 = 1$	$\phi(\boldsymbol{p},\boldsymbol{q},y) = \ln y - \dfrac{\alpha_1(\boldsymbol{q})}{\beta_{11}}\prod_{k\in J}p_k^{\beta_{kk}} - \sum_{\substack{k\in N\sim J\\ \beta_{kk}\neq 0}}\dfrac{\alpha_k(\boldsymbol{q})}{\beta_{kk}}p_k^{\beta_{kk}} - \sum_{\substack{k\in K\sim J\\ \beta_{kk}=0}}\alpha_k(\boldsymbol{q})\ln p_k$
(e8)-1	$\gamma_1 \neq 1$	$\phi(\boldsymbol{p},\boldsymbol{q},y) = \dfrac{y^{1-\gamma_1}}{1-\gamma_1} - \dfrac{\alpha_1(\boldsymbol{q})}{\beta_{11}}\prod_{k\in J}p_k^{\beta_{kk}} - \sum_{\substack{k\in N\sim J\\ \beta_{kk}\neq 0}}\dfrac{\alpha_k(\boldsymbol{q})}{\beta_{kk}}p_k^{\beta_{kk}} - \sum_{\substack{k\in K\sim J\\ \beta_{kk}=0}}\alpha_k(\boldsymbol{q})\ln p_k$
(e8)-2		$\phi(\boldsymbol{p},\boldsymbol{q},y) = y\prod_{k\in N\sim K}p_k^{-\beta_{kk}} - \dfrac{\alpha_1(\boldsymbol{q})}{\beta_{11}}\prod_{k\in J}p_k^{\beta_{kk}} - \sum_{\substack{k\in N\sim J\\ \beta_{kk}\neq 0}}\dfrac{\alpha_k(\boldsymbol{q})}{\beta_{kk}}p_k^{\beta_{kk}} - \sum_{\substack{k\in K\sim J\\ \beta_{kk}=0}}\alpha_k(\boldsymbol{q})\ln p_k$

Table 15
Quasi-Indirect Utility Functions for Restricted Incomplete Expenditure System Models

Model	Restrictions	Quasi-Indirect Utility Function
(s1)-1 & (s2)-1 & (s3)-1 & (s4)-1		$\phi(\mathbf{p},\mathbf{q},y) = y\prod_{k\in N} p_k^{-\alpha_k(\mathbf{q})} \exp\left\{-\sum_{k\in N}\beta_{kk}p_k\right\}$
		$\phi(\mathbf{p},\mathbf{q},y) = \ln y - \sum_{k\in N}\alpha_k(\mathbf{q})\ln p_k - \frac{1}{2}\sum_{k\in N}\sum_{j\in N}\beta_{kj}\ln p_k \ln p_j$
(s8)-1	$\gamma_1 = 0$	$\phi(\mathbf{p},\mathbf{q},y) = \ln y - \frac{\alpha_1(\mathbf{q})}{\beta_{11}}\prod_{k\in J}p_k^{\beta_{kk}} - \sum_{\substack{k\in N\sim J\\\beta_{kk}\neq 0}}\frac{\alpha_k(\mathbf{q})}{\beta_{kk}}p_k^{\beta_{kk}} - \sum_{\substack{k\in N\sim J\\\beta_{kk}=0}}\alpha_k(\mathbf{q})\ln p_k$
(s8)-1	$\gamma_1 \neq 0$	$\phi(\mathbf{p},\mathbf{q},y) = \frac{y^{-\gamma_1}}{-\gamma_1} - \frac{\alpha_1(\mathbf{q})}{\beta_{11}}\prod_{k\in J}p_k^{\beta_{kk}} - \sum_{\substack{k\in N\sim J\\\beta_{kk}\neq 0}}\frac{\alpha_k(\mathbf{q})}{\beta_{kk}}p_k^{\beta_{kk}} - \sum_{\substack{k\in N\sim J\\\beta_{kk}=0}}\alpha_k(\mathbf{q})\ln p_k$
(s8)-2		$\phi(\mathbf{p},\mathbf{q},y) = y\prod_{k\in N\sim K}p_k^{-\beta_{kk}} - \frac{\alpha_1(\mathbf{q})}{\beta_{11}}\prod_{k\in J}p_k^{\beta_{kk}} - \sum_{\substack{k\in K\sim J\\\beta_{kk}\neq 0}}\frac{\alpha_k(\mathbf{q})}{\beta_{kk}}p_k^{\beta_{kk}} - \sum_{\substack{k\in K\sim J\\\beta_{kk}=0}}\alpha_k(\mathbf{q})\ln p_k$

Technical Appendix

This appendix derives the necessary parameter restrictions for Slutsky symmetry to hold in an open neighborhood around observed prices and income. The approach employed is similar to LaFrance [1985, 1986]. For each of the 24 models, three mutually exclusive and exhaustive cases with alternative income effects for goods i and j ($i \neq j$) are considered: 1) no income effects, i.e., $\gamma_i = \gamma_j = 0$; 2) both goods having income effects, i.e., $\gamma_i \neq 0; \gamma_j \neq 0$; 2) only one good having income effects, ($\gamma_i \neq 0; \gamma_j = 0$). For each of these possibilities, the necessary parameter restrictions for Slutsky symmetry to hold regardless of prices and income were derived. Restrictions implied by the derivative properties of the Slutsky symmetry conditions were used extensively for this task. Once the parameter restrictions were identified for the three distinct income relationships, consistent combinations of the three sets of parameter restrictions were then determined.

1. The (x1) Model

Consider the (x1) unrestricted model specification:

$$x_i = \alpha_i(q) + \sum_{k=1}^{n} \beta_{ik} p_k + \gamma_i y \qquad (\text{x1})$$

The implied Slutsky symmetry conditions are:

$$\beta_{ji} + \gamma_j x_i = \beta_{ij} + \gamma_i x_j \qquad (1)$$

See LaFrance [1985] for the derivation of the necessary parameter restrictions.

2. The (x2) Model

Consider the (x2) unrestricted model specification:

$$x_i = \alpha_i(\boldsymbol{q}) + \sum_{k=1}^{n} \beta_{ik} p_k + \gamma_i \ln y \qquad (x2)$$

The implied Slutsky symmetry conditions are:

$$\beta_{ji} + \frac{\gamma_j}{y} x_i = \beta_{ij} + \frac{\gamma_i}{y} x_j \qquad (1)$$

The derivative of (1) with respect to p_k, $k = 1,\ldots, N$, implies the following restriction:

$$\gamma_j \beta_{ik} = \gamma_i \beta_{jk} \qquad (2)$$

The derivative of (1) with respect to y implies the following restriction:

$$\gamma_j x_i = \gamma_i x_j \qquad (3)$$

Case I. $\qquad \gamma_i = \gamma_j = 0$

- (1) implies:

$$\beta_{ji} = \beta_{ij} \qquad (4)$$

Case II. $\qquad \gamma_i \neq 0; \; \gamma_j \neq 0$

- (2) implies:

$$\beta_{jk} = (\gamma_j / \gamma_i)\beta_{ik}, \; \forall \, k \qquad (5)$$

- (3) and (5) together imply:

$$\alpha_j(\boldsymbol{q}) = (\gamma_j / \gamma_i)\alpha_i(\boldsymbol{q}) \qquad (6)$$

- Plugging (5) and (6) into (1) and simplifying implies:

$$\beta_{ij} = \beta_{ji} \qquad (7)$$

- One can combine (5) and (7) as:

$$\beta_{ij} = (\gamma_i \gamma_j / \gamma_k^2) \beta_{kk}, \forall k \tag{8}$$

- (6) and (8) jointly imply that:

$$\text{sgn}(\gamma_i) = \text{sgn}(\gamma_j) \neq 0 \tag{9}$$

- Thus, (6), (8), and (9) are the necessary parameter restrictions.

Case III. $\gamma_i \neq 0; \ \gamma_j = 0$

- (3) implies this case is only possible if $\gamma_i = 0$, a contradiction.

The restricted model specification takes the form:

1.
$$x_i = \alpha_i(q) + \sum_{k \in N} \beta_{ik} p_k, i \in N$$

2.
$$x_i = \frac{\gamma_i}{\gamma_1} \left\{ \alpha_1(q) + \frac{\beta_{11}}{\gamma_1} \sum_{k \in N} \gamma_k p_k + \gamma_1 \ln y \right\}, i \in N$$

3. The (x3) Model

Consider the (x3) unrestricted model specification:

$$x_i = \alpha_i(q) + \sum_{k=1}^{n} \beta_{ik} \ln p_k + \gamma_i y \tag{x3}$$

The implied Slutsky symmetry conditions are:

$$\frac{\beta_{ji}}{p_i} + \gamma_j x_i = \frac{\beta_{ij}}{p_j} + \gamma_i x_j \tag{1}$$

The derivative of (1) with respect to p_j implies:

$$-\beta_{ij} / p_j + \gamma_i \beta_{jj} = \gamma_j \beta_{ij} \tag{2}$$

Case I. $\gamma_i = \gamma_j = 0$

- (1) and (2) are only satisfied if:

$$\beta_{ij} = \beta_{ji} = 0 \tag{3}$$

Case II. $\gamma_i \neq 0; \ \gamma_j \neq 0$

- (2) holds in general only if:

$$\beta_{ik} = \beta_{jk} = 0, \forall k \tag{4}$$

- (4) and (1) imply:

$$\alpha_j(\boldsymbol{q}) = (\gamma_j / \gamma_i)\alpha_i(\boldsymbol{q}) \tag{5}$$

which further implies:

$$\text{sgn}(\gamma_i) = \text{sgn}(\gamma_j) \neq 0 \tag{6}$$

Case III. $\gamma_i \neq 0; \ \gamma_j = 0$

- (2) implies the restriction in (4), which with (1) implies $\gamma_i = 0$, a contradiction.

The restricted model specification takes the form:

1. $x_i = \alpha_i(\boldsymbol{q}) + \beta_{ii} \ln p_i, i \in N$

2. $x_i = (\gamma_i / \gamma_1)(\alpha_1(\boldsymbol{q}) + \gamma_1 y), i \in N$

4. The (x4) Model

Consider the (x4) unrestricted model specification:

$$x_i = \alpha_i(\boldsymbol{q}) + \sum_{k=1}^{n} \beta_{ik} \ln p_k + \gamma_i \ln y \tag{x4}$$

The implied Slutsky symmetry conditions are:

$$\frac{\beta_{ji}}{p_i} + \frac{\gamma_j}{y} x_i = \frac{\beta_{ij}}{p_j} + \frac{\gamma_i}{y} x_j \tag{1}$$

The derivative of (1) with respect to y implies:

$$\gamma_j x_i = \gamma_i x_j \tag{2}$$

Case I. $\gamma_i = \gamma_j = 0$

- (1) is satisfied only if:

$$\beta_{ij} = \beta_{ji} = 0 \tag{3}$$

Case II. $\gamma_i \neq 0;\ \gamma_j \neq 0$

- Plugging $x_j = (\gamma_j/\gamma_i)x_i$ from (2) into (1) implies (3). (3) and (2) along with the structure

  of (x4) imply the following three restrictions:

$$\beta_{ik} = \beta_{jk} = 0, \forall k \tag{4}$$

$$\alpha_j(\boldsymbol{q}) = (\gamma_j/\gamma_i)\alpha_i(\boldsymbol{q}) \tag{5}$$

$$\mathrm{sgn}(\gamma_i) = \mathrm{sgn}(\gamma_j) \neq 0 \tag{6}$$

Case III. $\gamma_i \neq 0;\ \gamma_j = 0$

- (2) implies $\gamma_i = 0$, a contradiction.

The restricted model specification takes the form:

1. $x_i = \alpha_i(\boldsymbol{q}) + \beta_{ii} \ln p_i, i \in N$

2. $x_i = (\gamma_i/\gamma_1)(\alpha_1(\boldsymbol{q}) + \gamma_1 \ln y), i \in N$

5. The (x5) Model

Consider the (x5) unrestricted model specification:

$$x_i = \alpha_i(q) \exp\left\{\sum_{k=1}^{n} \beta_{ik} p_k + \gamma_i y\right\} \tag{x5}$$

The implied Slutsky symmetry conditions are:

$$\beta_{ji} x_j + \gamma_j x_i x_j = \beta_{ij} x_i + \gamma_i x_i x_j \tag{1}$$

The derivative of (1) with respect to y implies:

$$\gamma_i s_{ij} = \gamma_j s_{ji} \tag{2}$$

The derivative of (1) with respect to p_k, $k=1,\ldots,N$, implies:

$$\beta_{ik}(s_{ij} - \gamma_j x_i x_j) = \beta_{jk}(s_{ji} - \gamma_i x_i x_j) \tag{3}$$

Case I. $\gamma_i = \gamma_j = 0$

- (1) implies $\beta_{ji} x_j = \beta_{ij} x_i$ which is satisfied only if:

$$\beta_{ij} = \beta_{ji} = 0 \tag{4}$$

or:

$$\beta_{ik} = \beta_{jk} = \beta_{kk}, \forall k \tag{5}$$

$$\alpha_i(q) = (\beta_{ii} / \beta_{jj}) \alpha_j(q) \tag{6}$$

Case II. $\gamma_i \neq 0; \gamma_j \neq 0$

- (2) implies $\gamma_i = \gamma_j$ and this case collapses into Case I above.

Case III. $\gamma_i \neq 0; \gamma_j = 0$

- (2) implies $s_{ij} = 0$. (1) implies that:

$$x_j = -\beta_{ij} / \gamma_i \tag{8}$$

The restricted model specification takes the form:

1.

$$x_i = \frac{\beta_{ii}}{\beta_{11}} \alpha_1(q) \exp\left\{\sum_{k \in J} \beta_{kk} p_k + \sum_{k \in N \sim K} \beta_{1k} p_k + \gamma_1 y\right\}, i \in J$$

$$x_i = \alpha_i(q) \exp\left\{\beta_{ii} p_i + \sum_{k \in N \sim K} \beta_{1k} p_k + \gamma_1 y\right\}, i \in K \sim J$$

$$x_i = -\beta_{1i} / \gamma_1, i \in N \sim K$$

Note that the subset $N \sim K$ is empty if $\gamma_1 = 0$.

6. *The (x6) Model*

Consider the (x6) unrestricted model specification:

$$x_i = \alpha_i(q) \exp\left\{\sum_{k=1}^{n} \beta_{ik} p_k\right\} y^{\gamma_i} \tag{x6}$$

The implied Slutsky symmetry conditions are:

$$\beta_{ji} x_j + \frac{\gamma_j}{y} x_i x_j = \beta_{ij} x_i + \frac{\gamma_i}{y} x_i x_j \tag{1}$$

The derivative of (1) with respect to y implies:

$$\gamma_i (s_{ij} - x_i x_j / y) = \gamma_j (s_{ji} - x_i x_j / y) \tag{2}$$

Case I. $\gamma_i = \gamma_j = 0$

- (1) simplifies to $\beta_{ji} x_j = \beta_{ij} x_i$. As with the (x5) model, this condition is satisfied only if:

$$\beta_{ij} = \beta_{ji} = 0 \tag{3}$$

- or:

$$\beta_{ik} = \beta_{jk} = \beta_{kk}, \forall k \tag{4}$$

$$\alpha_i(\boldsymbol{q}) = (\beta_{ii} / \beta_{jj})\alpha_j(\boldsymbol{q}) \tag{5}$$

Case II. $\gamma_i \neq 0; \ \gamma_j \neq 0$

- (2) implies $\gamma_i = \gamma_j$ or $s_{ij} = s_{ji} = x_i x_j / y$, but the later condition is only satisfied if

  $\gamma_i = \gamma_j = 1$ and $\beta_{ij} = \beta_{ji} = 0$. Thus, the following condition must hold:

$$\gamma_i = \gamma_j \tag{6}$$

- (6) implies $\beta_{ji} x_j = \beta_{ij} x_i$, and thus either the conditions in (3) or (4) and (5) must be

  satisfied.

Case III. $\gamma_i \neq 0; \ \gamma_j = 0$

- (2) implies that $s_{ij} = x_i x_j / y$, which when plugged back into (1) implies:

$$x_i = \beta_{ji} y \tag{7}$$

The restricted model specification takes the form:

1.
$$x_i = \frac{\beta_{ii}}{\beta_{11}} \alpha_1(\boldsymbol{q}) \exp\left\{ \sum_{k \in J} \beta_{kk} p_k \right\} y^{\gamma_1}, i \in J$$

$$x_i = \alpha_i(\boldsymbol{q}) \exp(\beta_{ii} p_i) y^{\gamma_1}, i \in N \sim J$$

2.
$$x_i = \frac{\beta_{ii}}{\beta_{11}} \alpha_1(\boldsymbol{q}) \exp\left\{ \sum_{k \in J} \beta_{kk} p_k + \sum_{k \in N \sim K} \beta_{1k} p_k \right\}, i \in J$$

$$x_i = \alpha_i(\boldsymbol{q}) \exp\left\{ \beta_{ii} p_i + \sum_{k \in N \sim K} \beta_{1k} p_k \right\}, i \in K \sim J$$

$$x_i = \beta_{1i} y, i \in N \sim K$$

7.   The (x7) Model

Consider the (x7) unrestricted model specification:

$$x_i = \alpha_i(\boldsymbol{q}) \prod_{k=1}^{n} p_k^{\beta_{ik}} \exp(\gamma_i y) \tag{x7}$$

The Slutsky symmetry conditions are:

$$\frac{\beta_{ji}}{p_i} x_j + \gamma_j x_i x_j = \frac{\beta_{ij}}{p_j} x_i + \gamma_i x_i x_j \tag{1}$$

The derivative of (1) with respect to y implies:

$$\gamma_j s_{ij} = \gamma_i s_{ji} \tag{2}$$

The derivative of (1) with respect to $p_k, k \neq i, j$, implies:

$$\beta_{jk}(s_{ji} - \gamma_i x_i x_j) = \beta_{ik}(s_{ij} - \gamma_j x_i x_j) \tag{3}$$

Case I. $\gamma_i = \gamma_j = 0$

- (1) simplifies to $\beta_{ji} p_j x_j = \beta_{ij} p_i x_i$, which is satisfied if:

$$\beta_{ij} = \beta_{ji} = 0 \tag{4}$$

- It can also be shown that (1) is satisfied if:

$$\beta_{kl} = 1 + \beta_{ll}, k = i, j; l = i, j; k \neq l \tag{5}$$

$$\beta_{jk} = \beta_{ik}, \forall k; k \neq i, j \tag{6}$$

$$\alpha_i(\boldsymbol{q}) = \frac{1 + \beta_{ii}}{1 + \beta_{jj}} \alpha_j(\boldsymbol{q}) \tag{7}$$

Case II. $\gamma_i \neq 0; \gamma_j \neq 0$

- (2) implies that $\gamma_i = \gamma_j$, and with this restriction the case collapses into Case I above.

Case III. $\gamma_i \neq 0;\ \gamma_j = 0$

- (2) implies that $s_{ji} = 0$, which is satisfied only if:

$$x_j = -(\beta_{ij} / \gamma_i) / p_j \tag{8}$$

The restricted model specification takes the form:

1.
$$x_i = \alpha_1(q)\left\{\frac{1+\beta_{ii}}{1+\beta_{11}}\right\}p_i^{-1}\prod_{k\in J}p_k^{1+\beta_{kk}}\prod_{k\in N\sim K}p_k^{\beta_{1k}}\exp(\gamma_1 y), i\in J$$

$$x_i = \alpha_i(q)p_i^{\beta_{ii}}\prod_{k\in N\sim K}p_k^{\beta_{1k}}\exp(\gamma_1 y), i\in K\sim J$$

$$x_i = -(\beta_{1i}/\gamma_1)p_i^{-1}, i\in N\sim K$$

Note that the $N\sim K$ set must be empty if $\gamma_1 = 0$.

8.   The (x8) Model

Consider the (x8) unrestricted model specification:

$$x_i = \alpha_i(q)\prod_{k=1}^{n}p_k^{\beta_{ik}}y^{\gamma_i} \tag{x8}$$

The Slutsky symmetry conditions are:

$$\frac{\beta_{ji}}{p_i}x_j + \frac{\gamma_j}{y}x_i x_j = \frac{\beta_{ij}}{p_j}x_i + \frac{\gamma_i}{y}x_i x_j \tag{1}$$

See LaFrance [1986] for the derivation of the necessary parameter restrictions.

9. The (e1) Model

Consider the (e1) unrestricted model specification:

$$e_i = \alpha_i(\boldsymbol{q}) + \sum_{k=1}^{N} \beta_{ik} p_k + \gamma_i y \tag{e1}$$

The implied Slutsky symmetry conditions are:

$$\frac{1}{p_i p_j}\{\beta_{ji} p_i + \gamma_j e_i\} = \frac{1}{p_i p_j}\{\beta_{ij} p_j + \gamma_i e_j\} \tag{1}$$

The derivative of (1) with respect to p_i implies:

$$\gamma_i \beta_{ji} = \beta_{ji} + \gamma_j \beta_{ii} \tag{2}$$

The derivative of (1) with respect to p_k, $k \neq i, j$, implies:

$$\gamma_j \beta_{ik} = \gamma_i \beta_{jk} \tag{3}$$

Case I. $\qquad \gamma_i = \gamma_j = 0$

- (1) and (2) imply:

$$\beta_{ij} = \beta_{ji} = 0 \tag{4}$$

Case II. $\qquad \gamma_i \neq 0; \ \gamma_j \neq 0$

- (3) implies:

$$\beta_{ik} = (\gamma_i / \gamma_j)\beta_{jk}, \ \forall \ k; \ k \neq i, j \tag{5}$$

- For (2) to hold it must be the case that:

$$\beta_{ii} = 0 \ \text{if} \ \gamma_i = 1 \tag{6}$$

$$\beta_{ji} = \frac{\gamma_j \beta_{ii}}{\gamma_i - 1} \ \text{if} \ \gamma_i \neq 1 \tag{7}$$

Thus, (5), (6), and (7) are the necessary parameter restrictions.

Case III. $\gamma_i \neq 0; \; \gamma_j = 0$

- (1) implies $e_j = -(\beta_{ij}/\gamma_i)p_j + (\beta_{ji}/\gamma_i)p_i$. Two possibilities are implied by this structure:

$$\gamma_i = 1 \; \& \; \beta_{jj} = -\beta_{ij} \;\; \Rightarrow \;\; e_j = -\beta_{ij}p_j + \beta_{ji}p_i \tag{9}$$

$$\gamma_i \neq 1 \; \& \; \beta_{ji} = 0 \;\; \Rightarrow \;\; e_j = -(\beta_{ij}/\gamma_i)p_j \tag{10}$$

The restricted model specification takes the form:

1. $e_i = \alpha_i(\boldsymbol{q}) + \beta_{ii}p_i, i \in N$

$$e_i = \alpha_1(\boldsymbol{q}) + \sum_{k \in K, i \neq k} \beta_{ik}p_k + \sum_{k \in N \sim K} \beta_{1k}p_k + y, i \in J$$

2. $e_i = \dfrac{\gamma_i}{\gamma_1}\alpha_1(\boldsymbol{q}) + \sum_{k \in K}\beta_{ik}p_k + \dfrac{\gamma_i}{\gamma_1}\sum_{k \in N \sim K}\beta_{1k}p_k + \gamma_i y, i \in K \sim J$

$e_i = -(\beta_{1i}/\gamma_1)p_i, i \in N \sim K$

3. $e_1 = \alpha_1(\boldsymbol{q}) + \sum_{k \in N}\beta_{1k}p_k + y$

$e_i = \beta_{i1}p_1 - \beta_{1i}p_i, i \in N, i \neq 1$

10. The (e2) Model

Consider the (e2) unrestricted model specification:

$$e_i = \alpha_i(\boldsymbol{q}) + \sum_{k=1}^{N}\beta_{ik}p_k + \gamma_i \ln y \tag{e2}$$

The implied Slutsky symmetry conditions are:

$$\frac{1}{p_i p_j}\left\{\beta_{ji}p_i + \frac{\gamma_j}{y}e_i\right\} = \frac{1}{p_i p_j}\left\{\beta_{ij}p_j + \frac{\gamma_i}{y}e_j\right\} \tag{1}$$

The derivative of (1) with respect to p_j implies:

$$\gamma_j \beta_{ij} / y = \beta_{ij} + \gamma_i \beta_{jj} / y \qquad (2)$$

The derivative of (1) with respect to p_k, $k \neq i, j$ implies:

$$\gamma_j \beta_{ik} = \gamma_i \beta_{jk} \qquad (3)$$

Case I. $\gamma_i = \gamma_j = 0$

- (2) implies:

$$\beta_{ij} = \beta_{ji} = 0 \qquad (4)$$

Case II. $\gamma_i \neq 0;\ \gamma_j \neq 0$

- (2) implies (4) must hold. (1), (2), and (4) imply:

$$\alpha_i(\boldsymbol{q}) = (\gamma_i / \gamma_j)\alpha_j(\boldsymbol{q}) \qquad (5)$$

$$\beta_{ik} = \beta_{jk} = 0, \forall\, k \qquad (6)$$

$$\mathrm{sgn}(\gamma_i) = \mathrm{sgn}(\gamma_j) \neq 0 \qquad (7)$$

Case III. $\gamma_i \neq 0;\ \gamma_j = 0$

- (1) implies $e_i = \dfrac{y}{\gamma_j}(\beta_{ij}p_j - \beta_{ji}p_i)$, which is inconsistent with (e2).

The restricted model specification implies:

1. $e_i = \alpha_i(\boldsymbol{q}) + \beta_{ii}p_i, i \in N$

2. $e_i = (\gamma_i / \gamma_1)(\alpha_1(\boldsymbol{q}) + \gamma_1 \ln y), i \in N$

11. The (e3) Model

Consider the (e3) unrestricted model specification:

$$e_j = \alpha_j(\boldsymbol{q}) + \sum_{j=1}^{N} \beta_{jk} \ln p_k + \gamma_j y \qquad (e3)$$

The implied Slutsky symmetry conditions are:

$$\frac{1}{p_i p_j} \{\beta_{ji} + \gamma_j e_i\} = \frac{1}{p_i p_j} \{\beta_{ij} + \gamma_i e_j\} \qquad (1)$$

The derivative of (1) with respect to p_k, $k=1,\ldots,N$, implies:

$$\gamma_j \beta_{ik} = \gamma_i \beta_{jk}, \ \forall \ i, j, k \qquad (2)$$

Case I. $\qquad \gamma_i = \gamma_j = 0$

- (1) implies:

$$\beta_{ji} = \beta_{ij} \qquad (3)$$

Case II. $\qquad \gamma_i \neq 0; \ \gamma_j \neq 0$

- (2) implies:

$$\beta_{ik} = \frac{\gamma_i}{\gamma_j} \beta_{jk}, \ \forall \ k \qquad (4)$$

- Plugging (4) back into (1) implies the following restriction:

$$\beta_{ji} - \beta_{ij} + \gamma_j \alpha_i(\boldsymbol{q}) + \gamma_i \alpha_j(\boldsymbol{q}) = 0 \qquad (5)$$

Case III. $\qquad \gamma_i \neq 0; \ \gamma_j = 0$

- (1) simplifies to $e_i = \beta_{ij}/\gamma_j - \beta_{ji}/\gamma_j$. To be consist with (e3), it must be the case that:

$$\beta_{ik} = 0, \ \forall k \qquad (6)$$

$$\alpha_i(\boldsymbol{q}) = -\beta_{ji}/\gamma_j \qquad (7)$$

The restricted model specification takes the form:

1. $\qquad e_i = \alpha_i(\boldsymbol{q}) + \sum_{k \in N} \beta_{ik} \ln p_k, i \in N$

$$2. \quad e_i = \frac{\gamma_i}{\gamma_1}\left\{\alpha_1(\boldsymbol{q}) - \frac{\beta_{1i}}{\gamma_i} + \frac{\beta_{i1}}{\gamma_i} + \sum_{k \in N}\beta_{1k}\ln p_k + \gamma_1 y\right\}, i \in J$$

$$e_i = -\beta_{1i}/\gamma_1, i \in N \sim J$$

12. The (e4) Model

Consider the (e4) unrestricted model specification:

$$e_i = \alpha_i(\boldsymbol{q}) + \sum_{k=1}^{N}\beta_{ik}\ln p_k + \gamma_i \ln y \tag{e4}$$

The implied Slutsky symmetry conditions are:

$$\frac{1}{p_i p_j}\left\{\beta_{ji} + \frac{\gamma_j}{y}e_i\right\} = \frac{1}{p_i p_j}\left\{\beta_{ij} + \frac{\gamma_i}{y}e_j\right\} \tag{1}$$

The derivative of (1) with respect to y implies:

$$\gamma_i e_j = \gamma_j e_i \tag{2}$$

The derivative of (1) with respect to p_k, $k=1,...,N$, implies:

$$\gamma_j \beta_{ik} = \gamma_i \beta_{jk}, \forall k \tag{3}$$

Case I. $\qquad \gamma_i = \gamma_j = 0$

- (1) implies:

$$\beta_{ji} = \beta_{ij} \tag{4}$$

Case II. $\qquad \gamma_i \neq 0; \ \gamma_j \neq 0$

- Plugging (2) into (1) and simplifying implies (4). (4) and (3) together imply:

$$\beta_{ij} = \frac{\gamma_i \gamma_j}{\gamma_k^2}\beta_{kk}, \forall k \tag{5}$$

$$\mathrm{sgn}(\gamma_i) = \mathrm{sgn}(\gamma_j) \neq 0 \tag{6}$$

- Plugging (5) back into (2) then implies:

$$\alpha_i(\boldsymbol{q}) = \frac{\gamma_i}{\gamma_j}\alpha_j(\boldsymbol{q}) \tag{7}$$

Case III. $\qquad \gamma_i \neq 0; \ \gamma_j = 0$

- (2) implies this case is not possible.

The restricted model specification implies:

1. $\qquad e_i = \alpha_i(\boldsymbol{q}) + \sum_{k \in N} \beta_{ik} \ln p_k, i \in N$

2. $\qquad e_i = \dfrac{\gamma_i}{\gamma_1}\left\{\alpha_1(\boldsymbol{q}) + \dfrac{\beta_{11}}{\gamma_1}\sum_{k \in N}\gamma_k \ln p_k + \gamma_1 \ln y\right\}, i \in N$

13. The (e5) Model

Consider the (e5) unrestricted model specification:

$$e_i = \alpha_i(\boldsymbol{q})\exp\left\{\sum_{k=1}^{n}\beta_{ik}p_k + \gamma_i y\right\} \tag{e5}$$

The Slutsky symmetry conditions are:

$$\frac{1}{p_i p_j}\left\{\beta_{ji}p_i e_j + \gamma_j e_i e_j\right\} = \frac{1}{p_i p_j}\left\{\beta_{ij}p_j e_i + \gamma_i e_i e_j\right\} \tag{1}$$

The derivative of (1) with respect to y implies:

$$\gamma_j s_{ji} = \gamma_i s_{ij} \tag{2}$$

Case I. $\gamma_i = \gamma_j = 0$

- (1) simplifies to $\beta_{ji} p_i e_j = \beta_{ij} p_j e_i$, which is not in general satisfied unless:

$$\beta_{ij} = \beta_{ji} \tag{3}$$

Case II. $\gamma_i \neq 0; \ \gamma_j \neq 0$

- (2) implies:

$$\gamma_i = \gamma_j \tag{4}$$

- (4) implies that (1) simplifies to $\beta_{ji} p_i e_j = \beta_{ij} p_j e_i$, and thus (3) must also be satisfied.

Case III. $\gamma_i \neq 0; \ \gamma_j = 0$

- (2) implies this case is not possible.

The restricted model specification takes the form:

1. $$e_i = \alpha_i(\boldsymbol{q}) \exp(\beta_{ii} p_i + \gamma_1 y), i \in N$$

14. The (e6) Model

Consider the (e6) unrestricted model specification:

$$e_i = \alpha_i(\boldsymbol{q}) \exp\left\{\sum_{k=1}^{n} \beta_{ik} p_k\right\} y^{\gamma_i} \tag{e6}$$

The Slutsky symmetry conditions are:

$$\frac{1}{p_i p_j}\left\{\beta_{ji} p_i e_j + \frac{\gamma_j}{y} e_i e_j\right\} = \frac{1}{p_i p_j}\left\{\beta_{ij} p_j e_i + \frac{\gamma_i}{y} e_i e_j\right\} \tag{1}$$

The derivative of (1) with respect to y implies:

$$\gamma_j \left\{ s_{ji} - \frac{e_j e_i}{p_j p_i y} \right\} = \gamma_i \left\{ s_{ij} - \frac{e_j e_i}{p_j p_i y} \right\} \tag{2}$$

Case I. $\qquad \gamma_i = \gamma_j = 0$

- (1) simplifies to $\beta_{ji} p_i e_j = \beta_{ij} p_j e_i$, which is not in general satisfied unless:

$$\beta_{ji} = \beta_{ij} \tag{3}$$

Case II. $\qquad \gamma_i \neq 0; \ \gamma_j \neq 0$

- (1) is not in general satisfied unless (3) and the following condition are satisfied:

$$\gamma_i = \gamma_j \tag{4}$$

Case III. $\qquad \gamma_i \neq 0; \ \gamma_j = 0$

- (2) implies that $s_{ij} = e_j e_i / (p_j p_i y)$. This restriction along with (1) implies $e_i = \beta_{ji} p_i y$, which is inconsistent with (e6).

The restricted model specification implies:

1. $\qquad\qquad e_i = \alpha_i(\boldsymbol{q}) \exp(\beta_{ii} p_i) y^{\gamma_1}, i \in N$

15. *The (e7) Model*

Consider the (e7) unrestricted model specification:

$$e_i = \alpha_i(\boldsymbol{q}) \prod_{k=1}^{n} p_k^{\beta_{ik}} \exp(\gamma_i y) \tag{e7}$$

The Slutsky symmetry conditions are:

$$\frac{1}{p_i p_j} \left\{ \beta_{ji} e_j + \gamma_j e_i e_j \right\} = \frac{1}{p_i p_j} \left\{ \beta_{ij} e_i + \gamma_i e_i e_j \right\} \tag{1}$$

The derivative of (1) with respect to y implies:

$$\gamma_j s_{ji} = \gamma_i s_{ij} \tag{2}$$

Case I. $\gamma_i = \gamma_j = 0$

- In this case, (1) simplifies to $\beta_{ji} e_j = \beta_{ij} e_i$, which is satisfied only if:

$$\beta_{ij} = \beta_{ji} = 0 \tag{3}$$

  or:

$$\beta_{jk} = \beta_{ik}, \forall k \tag{4}$$

$$\alpha_i(\boldsymbol{q}) = \frac{\beta_{ii}}{\beta_{jj}} \alpha_j(\boldsymbol{q}) \tag{5}$$

Case II. $\gamma_i \neq 0; \ \gamma_j \neq 0$

- (2) implies:

$$\gamma_i = \gamma_j \tag{6}$$

- Using (6), (1) simplifies to $\beta_{ji} e_j = \beta_{ij} e_i$, which is satisfied only if (3) or (4) and (5) are

  satisfied.

Case III. $\gamma_i \neq 0; \ \gamma_j = 0$

- (2) implies this case is not possible unless $s_{ij} = 0$,

  which holds only if:

$$e_j = -\beta_{ij} / \gamma_i \tag{7}$$

The restricted model specification takes the form:

$$e_i = (\beta_{ii}/\beta_{11})\alpha_1(\boldsymbol{q})\prod_{k\in J} p_k^{\beta_{kk}} \prod_{k\in N\sim K} p_k^{\beta_{1k}} \exp(\gamma_1 y), i \in J$$

$$\textbf{1.} \qquad e_i = \alpha_i(\boldsymbol{q})p_i^{\beta_{ii}} \prod_{k\in N\sim K} p_k^{\beta_{1k}} \exp(\gamma_1 y), i \in K \sim J$$

$$e_i = -(\beta_{1i}/\gamma_1), i \in N \sim K$$

16. The (e8) Model

Consider the (e8) unrestricted model specification:

$$e_i = \alpha_i(\boldsymbol{q})\prod_{k=1}^{n} p_k^{\beta_{ik}} y^{\gamma_i} \tag{e8}$$

The Slutsky symmetry conditions are:

$$\frac{1}{p_i p_j}\left\{\beta_{ji}e_j + \frac{\gamma_j}{y}e_i e_j\right\} = \frac{1}{p_i p_j}\left\{\beta_{ij}e_i + \frac{\gamma_i}{y}e_i e_j\right\} \tag{1}$$

This model is equivalent to (x8). See LaFrance [1986] for the derivation of the necessary parameter restrictions.

17. The (s1) Model

Consider the (s1) unrestricted model specification:

$$s_i = \alpha_i(\boldsymbol{q}) + \sum_{k=1}^{n} \beta_{ik}p_k + \gamma_i y \tag{s1}$$

The implied Slutsky symmetry conditions are:

$$\frac{y}{p_i p_j}\left\{\beta_{ji}p_i + (s_j + \gamma_j y)s_i\right\} = \frac{y}{p_i p_j}\left\{\beta_{ij}p_j + (s_i + \gamma_i y)s_j\right\} \tag{1}$$

Case I. $\qquad \gamma_i = \gamma_j = 0$

- (1) simplifies in this case to $\beta_{ji} p_i = \beta_{ij} p_j$, which is satisfied only if:

$$\beta_{ij} = \beta_{ji} = 0 \qquad (2)$$

Case II. $\qquad \gamma_i \neq 0; \ \gamma_j \neq 0$

- (1) simplifies to $\beta_{ji} p_i + \gamma_j y s_i = \beta_{ij} p_j + \gamma_i y s_j$ which when differentiated with respect to y

implies $\gamma_j s_i = \gamma_i s_j$, and when differentiated with respect to p_i implies

$\beta_{ji}(1 - \gamma_i y) = -\gamma_j y \beta_{ii}$. These two conditions hold in general only if:

$$\beta_{ik} = \beta_{jk} = 0, k = i, j \qquad (3)$$

Case III. $\qquad \gamma_i \neq 0; \ \gamma_j = 0$

- (1) in this case simplifies to $s_i = (\beta_{ij} p_j - \beta_{ji} p_i)/(\gamma_j y)$, which is inconsistent with the

structure of (s1).

The restricted model specification takes the form:

1. $\qquad\qquad s_i = \alpha_i(\boldsymbol{q}) + \beta_{ii} p_i, i \in N$

2. $\qquad\qquad s_i = (\gamma_i / \gamma_1)(\alpha_1(\boldsymbol{q}) + \gamma_1 y), i \in N$

18. The (s2) Model

Consider the (s2) unrestricted model specification:

$$s_i = \alpha_i(\boldsymbol{q}) + \sum_{k=1}^{n} \beta_{ik} p_k + \gamma_i \ln y \qquad (s2)$$

The implied Slutsky symmetry conditions are:

$$\frac{y}{p_i p_j}\left\{\beta_{ji}p_i + (s_j + \gamma_j)s_i\right\} = \frac{y}{p_i p_j}\left\{\beta_{ij}p_j + (s_i + \gamma_i)s_j\right\} \tag{1}$$

Case I. $\qquad \gamma_i = \gamma_j = 0$

- (1) simplifies in this case to $\beta_{ji}p_i = \beta_{ij}p_j$, which is satisfied only if:

$$\beta_{ij} = \beta_{ji} = 0 \tag{2}$$

Case II. $\qquad \gamma_i \neq 0;\ \gamma_j \neq 0$

- (1) simplifies to $\beta_{ji}p_i + \gamma_j s_i = \beta_{ij}p_j + \gamma_i s_j$ whose derivative with respect to p_i is

$\beta_{ji}(\gamma_i - 1) = \gamma_j \beta_{ii}$ and whose derivative with respect to p_k, $k \neq i, j$, is $\gamma_j \beta_{ik} = \gamma_i \beta_{jk}$.

For these conditions to hold in general, either:

$$\gamma_i = 1 \tag{3}$$

$$\beta_{ii} = 0 \tag{4}$$

$$\beta_{ik} = \beta_{jk}/\gamma_j, \ \forall\ k;\ k \neq i, j \tag{5}$$

or:

$$\gamma_i \neq 1 \tag{7}$$

$$\beta_{ji} = \frac{\gamma_j \beta_{ii}}{\gamma_i - 1} \tag{8}$$

Case III. $\qquad \gamma_i \neq 0;\ \gamma_j = 0$

- (1) in this case simplifies to $s_i = (\beta_{ij}p_j - \beta_{ji}p_i)/\gamma_j$. To be consistent with (e2), this

condition requires that either:

$$\gamma_j = 1 \tag{9}$$

or:

$$\beta_{ij} = 0 \qquad (10)$$

The restricted model specification takes the form:

1. $$s_i = \alpha_i(\boldsymbol{q}) + \beta_{ii} p_i, i \in N$$

$$s_i = \alpha_1(\boldsymbol{q}) + \sum_{k \in K, i \neq k} \beta_{ik} p_k + \sum_{k \in N \sim K} \beta_{1k} p_k + \ln y, i \in J$$

2. $$s_i = \frac{\gamma_i}{\gamma_1} \alpha_1(\boldsymbol{q}) + \sum_{k \in K} \beta_{ik} p_k + \frac{\gamma_i}{\gamma_1} \sum_{k \in N \sim K} \beta_{1k} p_k + \gamma_i \ln y, i \in K \sim J$$

$$s_i = -(\beta_{1i} / \gamma_1) p_i, i \in N \sim K$$

3. $$s_1 = \alpha_1(\boldsymbol{q}) + \sum_{k \in N} \beta_{1k} p_k + \ln y$$

$$s_i = \beta_{i1} p_1 - \beta_{1i} p_i, i \in N, i \neq 1$$

19. The (s3) Model

Consider the (s3) unrestricted model specification:

$$s_i = \alpha_i(\boldsymbol{q}) + \sum_{k=1}^{n} \beta_{ik} \ln p_k + \gamma_i y \qquad (s3)$$

The implied Slutsky symmetry conditions are:

$$\frac{y}{p_i p_j} \left\{ \beta_{ji} + (s_j + \gamma_j y) s_i \right\} = \frac{y}{p_i p_j} \left\{ \beta_{ij} + (s_i + \gamma_i y) s_j \right\} \qquad (1)$$

Case I. $\qquad \gamma_i = \gamma_j = 0$

- (1) implies:

$$\beta_{ij} = \beta_{ji} \qquad (2)$$

Case II. $\gamma_i \neq 0;\ \gamma_j \neq 0$

- The derivative of (1) with respect to p_k, $k=1,...,N$, implies:

$$\beta_{ik} = \frac{\gamma_i}{\gamma_j}\beta_{jk} \tag{3}$$

- Plugging (3) into (1) implies:

$$\alpha_i(\boldsymbol{q}) = \frac{\gamma_i}{\gamma_j}\alpha_j(\boldsymbol{q}) \tag{4}$$

$$\beta_{ij} = \beta_{ji} \tag{5}$$

- (3) and (5) can be combined as follows:

$$\beta_{ij} = \frac{\gamma_i\gamma_j}{\gamma_k^2}\beta_{kk},\ \forall k \tag{6}$$

- Thus, (4) and (6) are the necessary restrictions for this case.

Case III. $\gamma_i \neq 0;\ \gamma_j = 0$

- (1) simplifies to $s_i = (-\beta_{ji} + \beta_{ij})/\gamma_j y$, which is inconsistent with (s3).

The restricted model specification takes the form:

1. $$s_i = \alpha_i(\boldsymbol{q}) + \sum_{k \in N}\beta_{ik}\ln p_k, i \in N$$

2. $$s_i = \frac{\gamma_i}{\gamma_1}\left\{\alpha_1(\boldsymbol{q}) + \frac{\beta_{11}}{\gamma_1}\sum_{k \in N}\gamma_k\ln p_k + \gamma_1 y\right\}, i \in N$$

20. The (s4) Model

Consider the (s4) unrestricted model specification:

$$s_i = \alpha_i(\boldsymbol{q}) + \sum_{k=1}^{n} \beta_{ik} \ln p_k + \gamma_i \ln y \qquad \text{(s4)}$$

The implied Slutsky symmetry conditions are:

$$\frac{y}{p_i p_j}\left\{\beta_{ji} + (s_j + \gamma_j)s_i\right\} = \frac{y}{p_i p_j}\left\{\beta_{ij} + (s_i + \gamma_i)s_j\right\} \qquad (1)$$

Case I. $\gamma_i = \gamma_j = 0$

- (1) implies:

$$\beta_{ij} = \beta_{ji} \qquad (2)$$

Case II. $\gamma_i \neq 0;\ \gamma_j \neq 0$

- The derivative of (1) with respect to p_k, $k = 1,\dots,N$, implies:

$$\beta_{ik} = \frac{\gamma_i}{\gamma_j}\beta_{jk},\ \forall k \qquad (3)$$

- Plugging (3) into (1) implies:

$$\alpha_i(\boldsymbol{q}) = \frac{\gamma_i}{\gamma_j}\left\{\alpha_j(\boldsymbol{q}) - \frac{\beta_{ji}}{\gamma_i} + \frac{\beta_{ij}}{\gamma_i}\right\} \qquad (4)$$

Case III. $\gamma_i \neq 0;\ \gamma_j = 0$

- (1) implies $s_i = (\beta_{ij} - \beta_{ji})/\gamma_j$, but the structure of (s4) requires that:

$$\beta_{ij} = 0 \qquad (5)$$

The restricted model specification takes the form:

1. $s_i = \alpha_i(\boldsymbol{q}) + \sum_{k \in N} \beta_{ik} \ln p_k,\ i \in N$

2. $$s_i = \frac{\gamma_i}{\gamma_1}\left\{\frac{\beta_{i1}}{\gamma_i} - \frac{\beta_{1i}}{\gamma_i} + \alpha_1(q) + \sum_{k \in N}\beta_{1k}\ln p_k + \gamma_1 \ln y\right\}, i \in J$$

$$s_i = -\beta_{1i}/\gamma_1, i \in N \sim J$$

21. The (s5) Model

Consider the (s5) unrestricted model specification:

$$s_i = \alpha_i(q)\exp\left\{\sum_{k=1}^{n}\beta_{ik}p_k + \gamma_i y\right\} \tag{s5}$$

The implied Slutsky symmetry conditions are:

$$\frac{y}{p_i p_j}\left\{\beta_{ji}p_i s_j + (1+\gamma_j y)s_i s_j\right\} = \frac{y}{p_i p_j}\left\{\beta_{ij}p_j s_i + (1+\gamma_i y)s_i s_j\right\} \tag{1}$$

The derivative of (1) with respect to y implies:

$$(1/y + \gamma_j)s_{ji} = (1/y + \gamma_i)s_{ij} \tag{2}$$

Case I. $\gamma_i = \gamma_j = 0$

- (1) simplifies to $\beta_{ji}p_i s_j = \beta_{ij}p_j s_i$, which holds in general only if:

$$\beta_{ij} = \beta_{ji} = 0 \tag{3}$$

Case II. $\gamma_i \neq 0$; $\gamma_j \neq 0$

- (1) and (2) imply that:

$$\gamma_i = \gamma_j \tag{4}$$

- Given (4), (1) simplifies to $\beta_{ji}p_i s_j = \beta_{ij}p_j s_i$. As a result, (3) must also hold.

Case III. $\gamma_i \neq 0$; $\gamma_j = 0$

- (2) requires that $\gamma_i = 0$, a contradiction.

The restricted model specification takes the form:

1.
$$s_i = \alpha_i(\boldsymbol{q})\exp(\beta_{ii}p_i + \gamma_1 y), i \in N$$

22. The (s6) Model

Consider the (s6) unrestricted model specification:

$$s_i = \alpha_i(\boldsymbol{q})\exp\left\{\sum_{k=1}^{n}\beta_{ik}p_k\right\}y^{\gamma_i} \tag{s6}$$

The implied Slutsky symmetry conditions are:

$$\frac{y}{p_i p_j}\left\{\beta_{ji}p_i s_j + (1+\gamma_j)s_i s_j\right\} = \frac{y}{p_i p_j}\left\{\beta_{ij}p_j s_i + (1+\gamma_i)s_i s_j\right\} \tag{1}$$

The derivative of (1) with respect to y implies:

$$(s_{ji} - s_{ij})/y + \gamma_j\beta_{ji}s_j/p_j - \gamma_i\beta_{ij}s_i/p_i + (\gamma_j^2 - \gamma_i^2)s_i s_j/(p_i p_j) = 0 \tag{2}$$

Case I. $\gamma_i = \gamma_j = 0$

- (1) becomes $\beta_{ji}p_i s_j = \beta_{ij}p_j s_i$, which holds in general only if :

$$\beta_{ij} = \beta_{ji} = 0 \tag{3}$$

Case II. $\gamma_i \neq 0;\ \gamma_j \neq 0$

- (1) simplifies to $\beta_{ji}p_i/s_i + \gamma_j = \beta_{ij}p_j/s_j + \gamma_i$, which along with (2) is generally satisfied

  only if (3) and the following condition hold:

$$\gamma_i = \gamma_j \tag{4}$$

Case III. $\gamma_i \neq 0; \ \gamma_j = 0$

- There are no parameter restrictions under which (1) and (2) hold unless $\gamma_i = 0$, a

    contradiction.

The restricted model specification takes the form:

1. $$s_i = \alpha_i(\boldsymbol{q})\exp(\beta_{ii}p_i)y^{\gamma_1}, i \in N$$

23. *The (s7) Model*

Consider the (s7) unrestricted model specification:

$$s_i = \alpha_i(\boldsymbol{q})\prod_{k=1}^{n} p_k^{\beta_{ik}} \exp(\gamma_i y) \tag{s7}$$

The implied Slutsky symmetry conditions are:

$$\frac{y}{p_i p_j}\left\{\beta_{ji}s_j + (1+\gamma_j y)s_i s_j\right\} = \frac{y}{p_i p_j}\left\{\beta_{ij}s_i + (1+\gamma_i y)s_i s_j\right\} \tag{1}$$

The derivative of (1) with respect to y implies:

$$(1/y + \gamma_j)s_{ji} = (1/y + \gamma_i)s_{ij} \tag{2}$$

Case I. $\gamma_i = \gamma_j = 0$

- (1) simplifies to $\beta_{ji}s_j = \beta_{ij}s_i$, which in general holds either if:

$$\beta_{ij} = \beta_{ji} = 0 \tag{3}$$

    or:

$$\beta_{jk} = \beta_{ik}, \forall k \tag{4}$$

$$\alpha_i(\boldsymbol{q}) = \frac{\beta_{ii}}{\beta_{jj}}\alpha_j(\boldsymbol{q}) \tag{5}$$

Case II. $\quad \gamma_i \neq 0; \ \gamma_j \neq 0$

- (2) implies:

$$\gamma_i = \gamma_j \tag{6}$$

- With (6), (1) simplifies to $\beta_{ji}s_j = \beta_{ij}s_i$, which implies either (3) or (4) and (5) must also

  hold.

Case III. $\quad \gamma_i \neq 0; \ \gamma_j = 0$

- (2) implies $\gamma_i = 0$, a contradiction.

The restricted model specification takes the form:

1.
$$s_i = (\beta_{ii}/\beta_{11})\alpha_1(\boldsymbol{q})\prod_{k \in J} p_k^{\beta_{kk}}\exp(\gamma_1 y), i \in J$$
$$s_i = \alpha_i(\boldsymbol{q})p_i^{\beta_{ii}}\exp(\gamma_1 y), i \in N \sim J$$

24. The (s8) Model

Consider the (s8) unrestricted model specification:

$$s_i = \alpha_i(\boldsymbol{q})\prod_{k=1}^{n} p_k^{\beta_{ik}} y^{\gamma_i} \tag{s8}$$

The implied Slutsky symmetry conditions are:

$$\frac{y}{p_i p_j}\left\{\beta_{ji}s_j + (1+\gamma_j)s_i s_j\right\} = \frac{y}{p_i p_j}\left\{\beta_{ij}s_i + (1+\gamma_i)s_i s_j\right\} \tag{1}$$

This model is identical to the (x8) and (e8) models up to a parametric transformation. See LaFrance [1986] for a derivation of the necessary parameter restrictions.